The Magical power of
Your Name and The Numbers
you use according to the
Laws of Attraction

The Magical power of Your Name and The Numbers you use according to the Laws of attraction

Your names and numbers count! Wisely and richly it attracts the life you truly want 4ever!

Asnat Almaliah Frey

Published 10/09/2013

ISBN-13: 978-1492873419

ISBN-10: 1492873411

Library of Congress Control Number: Pending

Contents

Your name and the names you use for yourself and others are codes. They *count* and attract what makes and keep you happy, healthy, successful, and wealthy, thanks to the wonderful laws of attraction.

Dedication

First, I dedicate this book to my wonderful, loving, caring and powerful creators: my wonderful and loving parents, Aliza and Prosper Almaliah and God — Hashem, the powerful, loving, caring, wonderful, nurturing, abundant and provider almighty.

Second, I dedicate this book to my wonderful and loving family, clients, and friends as well as to all the many people who has helped and helping me and my books help the many millions of wonderful people of this universe.

Also, I dedicate this book to all my great teachers i have been blessed by. I love, thank and appreciate each and one of you!

Acknowledgments

First, I thank God—Hashem, for the energy love and abundant supply thanks to which I achieve my goals rightfully and magically with joy and ease and with success way greater than my own beliefs. Second, I thank my wonderful parents, Aliza and Prosper Elimelech, my children, Shir Lior and Moshe Frey, my loving fiance Ofir Chazut, and his family and friends, (especially, Yocheved Yonayov, Amira Yonayov, Ayelet and Efraim Nahum, Rachel and Gai Sade, Elad and Miri Chazut, Matan Chazut) my brother, Doron Elimelech, my sister, Keren lugasi andtheir magnificent families.

A special thank you goes out to all the many wonderful, loving, and successful clients of mine. I thank them for their trust in me, my teachings and talents as well as for achieving their goals rightfully, with love and ease by applying the guidance and principals included in my different coaching sessions and products.

In addition, I thank the many wonderful, successful, professionals, creative, powerful, supporting and talented people for recognizing my talents, purpose and passion as well as, for their trust and help in achieving my goal; helping and guiding, through my books, products, services, talents, shows in the media, all of you millions of wonderful people of this universe who wish to use the law of attraction the right way and enjoy a good, wealthy, healthy, loving productive and successful life with huge success, joy and ease.

Part I

Your name and the names
You use for Yourself or others
create and attract

Your name—your code and call

When God created man in His image, He called him *man,* and at that moment, He gave man certain characteristics and energies as his purpose and calling.

Let's take a good look at the letters of the word m-a-n. Now read the word backward. What do you see? Yes! N-a-m (e)! Surprised?

What was one of the first things your parents did when you were born? They gave you a *name.* At that moment, your identity and purpose was determined for you. Why? What is in a name? Whether you choose to believe it or not, your name counts more than most people know.

The simple combination of letters and sounds not only defines your basic character, energy, and purpose in life but also delivers a hidden yet clear message. It is equally responsible for the spiritual realm in terms of your spiritual qualities.

Our name sums up our past, our present, and our future. It represents the very essence of our soul. It predetermines the type and qualities of our physical body and the way the soul expresses itself in the material world. We base this on many factors, such as the intention behind one's name as well as the quantity, the sequence, and the type of letters that comprise our name. Therefore, changing one letter of our name will result in changes in how our soul vibrates. The *name* of a person is like the blueprint of a man. It contains all the right information and instructions as to how the soul is built. Just like any blueprint, if you want to upgrade or modify it, you will need to go into the plans and see how and where you are able to modify. In other words, a name contains the DNA of the given object or person in strict correlation to universal energy vibration.

Choosing a right and good name for our offspring is a very important decision.

The majority of parents choose a name because of their love of a family member, a movie star, or a sports player. Others choose a name from a list of biblical figures; some even choose to name their child after a deceased loved one out of respect and with the desire to keep the name alive. Some creative parents will hyphenate both their names to create a new name. Others choose according to cultural trend or background.

A very small percentage of the population chooses their child's name based on the energy traits that are contained in the name. (The energy in each letter that composes the child's name, the numeric value of each letter, the total sum of the letters combined, or the history or origins of the name, and finally, the meaning of its intention.) Very few parents go through the proper steps wholly and absolutely conscious that this chosen name will determine their child's future personality.

As you know, my name is Osnat, and for a short period, people used to call me Ozzie for short. I allowed it, for it was easier to pronounce. My friends liked to call me Ozzie because it sounded sweeter. My ex-husband, on the other hand, used to call me "Ossnat," and although it may sound similar (he had added an *s*), it actually resulted in a change to the energy.

In order to understand this concept better, try this exercise: ask someone close to you to call you with a different name and *feel* the energy change. Now try calling someone you know very well with a different name (perhaps a nickname), and witness the shift of energy within you first, and then notice your energy toward that person. Even though both of you are the same person, a change resulted from the *name* by which you now call that person.

In Judaism, God has many names. According to the Kabbalah, there is an additional set of seventy-two names, and each name is composed of three letters. Each letter has its own specific character and identity. Each combination reflects or calls on a specific energy or, in other words, a specific attribute of God. Separately, they highlight only the specific character trait while the seventy-two names together represent perfection.

In the Hebrew language, when a person wants to talk about God, he will use the common name Hashem, which means *The Name*. *Ha* means "the" and *shem* means "name." Therefore, Hashem calls on the energy from one or more of the seventy-two names or attributes of God according to the personal intention of the speaker. The name Hashem is indicative of various character traits of God, in fact, the ones you intentionally choose to call.

You may already know that words call or connect to a specific energy. Consequently, knowing the energy of your name and who, if anyone, you were named after is powerful, positive, enriching, and rewarding because your name affects every aspect of your life.

The Mirror Law

In Hebrew, there is a famous phrase that when translated states, "And you should love your friend like yourself." Can you see the catch to that phrase? Let me explain. How can we love, respect, and treat others in a loving, respectful, and understanding way if we do not know how to love, respect, and understand ourselves? We should start to love, respect, understand, and appreciate ourselves first. The moment we begin to love, respect, nurture, and understand our self, we will love, respect, nurture, understand, and appreciate others naturally and easily.

There is another point to ponder. How can we love and understand ourselves if we do not know who we are and what we are made of? What is our purpose in life? What are our desires? What are our deepest dreams? What makes us feel good? If we do not know the answers to these important questions, how then can we expect to know how to respect others and their rights to form their own opinions, desires, thoughts, actions, and personal life choices?

Before we give, share, understand, praise, and even love others, we start with ourselves. So now back to our question, *who are we*?

There are many theories behind that basic question. In my opinion, the most important information about ourselves is the knowledge that everything in this universe is energy, such as ourselves—we are energy based on our energy codes.

Well, what are the codes? Everything we see is a type of code made up of letters that translate into numbers. These numbers are a type of DNA that creates the actual object. Thus, our name is the translated numbers from these specified codes. Since every part of us is a reflection of a number—the code—it carries particular characteristics. We need to look at the energies that form and shape us, such as those formed by our names (letters that translate to numbers) and birth dates (numbers).

In further chapters, we will discuss other frequencies that may be influencing our energies, such as our homes, cars, and offices, as well as hotel rooms and places we lodge.

Furthermore, I place my belief in the theory that before we were born into this world, we had a plan. We came for a specific purpose to achieve certain and specific outcomes. Or we simply came to become who we were meant to become in life, and the memory of that positive and important mission is pushing, guiding, and directing us.

In order to fulfill that purpose, we chose specific traits: our birth date, name, country, city, town, and maybe even our siblings and parents. The way I describe this to people is that we were born with a set program. This program is continuously running in perfect order in "God's computer." First, it runs according to the chosen codes such as the name, birth date, etc., and then, when we gain awareness of our traits and personal power (according to the codes), we consciously choose our words, thoughts, beliefs, and actions to achieve and fulfill our mission in life positively, rightfully, and successfully.

Great! Now you know every word you express to yourself or to others (yes, even mentally) is actually a name. This name has specific traits and energy and goes out to the universe to work for you. I know you will use this wisdom wisely and enjoy positive and desired outcomes in *your* life and that of the people you love.

Awareness of this ancient wisdom is beneficial to you since your name and the names you give others affect every aspect of your life. Call on all the right, good, desired, and blessed energy by simply choosing your words. The names you give to people and things, and the energy you create by it, will take place automatically and will work for you.

Let us first find out what our codes are. Then we will take a glimpse into our basic characteristics, some of our likes and dislikes, and our purpose as well as the things we want or have in this chosen lifetime.

In the following pages, you will find detailed information regarding every letter and number that composes your energy.

Numerology!

Here we will look at some of our energy codes and discover the main traits and how they may affect us in our lives.

The first and most important ones are your name, your birth date, and the codes of the people you are in a relationship with. Then we will look at the traits of the energy codes of any given space you are in, such as your home, work, business, car, airplane, ship, etc. The energies may work for you directly or indirectly.

Even a seat in an airplane, train, boat, etc., has a specific energy—traits according to its numeric code and is manifested according to the great law of attraction as well as that of creativity. These codes awaken to action and manifest in the physical world as soon as they are used. The important and detailed information shared in this book will help you to use these codes wisely so you can achieve all your goals in a fast and easy way.

In the following pages, I will explain in detail how it works and what the main traits of each code are.

You may wish to take out a pen and paper to calculate some important energy numbers in your life.

the first Codes
the letters that Compose
our Name

A

---

its numeric value is 1

- Is all about being number one

- Represents the masculine gender and the father figure

- Desires and strives for love, yet also knows how to give it

- Is mainly spiritual and often deals with faith and self-growth

- Is extremely curious and is in constant pursuit of the truth since faith is the essence of the letter A

- Represents the beginning of things

- Desires to stand out and lead others and is often competitive and successful

- Looks to unite everything and everyone

- Relates to parenting and protecting

- If pressed upon, will compromise for peace and truth

B

---

its numeric value is 2

- Represents the feminine gender and is naturally intuitive, sensitive, nurturing, fertile, fruitful, prosperous, and creative
- Relates to home and family
- Big and blessed and represents abundance and prosperity
- Is often associated with motherhood and the energy of giving birth
- Productive, active, wise, diplomatic, and somewhat manipulative
- Admires beauty and best behavior
- Constantly grows and builds
- At times emotional, which may lead to overeating and over nurturing
- Possesses strong need for clarity

C

---

its numeric value is 3

- Open character and looks for freedom and free space

- Represents expansion in all areas of life, mainly wealth, knowledge, traveling, and distances

- Manifests abundance and great luck (being at the right place at the right time and with the right intention)

- Enjoys nature, climbing, exploring, traveling, and expanding in every area of life without focus

- Inspired and driven

- Judgmental and opinionated

- Genuinely loving, caring, warm, joyful, honest, generous, and always a winner when taking chances

D

its numeric value is 4

- Represents wealth or poverty, beginnings or endings

- Represents the need and desire for constant change and being unique

- Productive yet always finds ways to be original and different (likes diversity and change)

- Disconnected from the past and relates mainly to the future, modernization, technology, and advancement

- Easily preoccupied about the future and needs to learn to worry less

- Brave and always looks to reach new levels of success

- Has the ability to rise and succeed in whatever the choice may be, as long as it opens the right door

- Looks independent on the outside but is extremely dependent on others, especially for love

- Demanding, energetic, and can be high tempered

E

its numeric value is 5

- Excellent communicator

- Has great leadership skills, is unique and wise

- Flexible and at times manipulative

- Social, charismatic, and an excellent negotiator

- Joyful and playful with others

- Bored easily and therefore deals with different things simultaneously

- Able to understand and work with elaborate or complex information and clearly communicate it to others

- Knowledgeable and talented

- Connected to different spiritual worlds and realms

F

its numerical value is 8

- Is fruitful, profit orientated, and open to prosperity
- Always relates to leadership, power, and control
- Looks forward to the future in a positive and profitable way
- Traditional and even somewhat religious
- Has amazing social skills
- Flirtatious, friendly, and a great friend to have
- Respecting and loving
- A successful communicator
- Physically strong
- Fancy, fabulous, and fair
- Driven by speed and profits
- Seeks to achieve high rank and fame

G

---

its numerical value is 3

- Relates to growth and learning

- Genuine and wise

- Loves people and is loved by many

- A generous giver and taker

- Relates to others in a unique, charismatic, and understanding way

- Diplomatic, quiet, and observant

- Able to see beyond the present situation

- Tall and relates to spaces and heights

- Simple, modest, direct, and honest

H

---

its numeric value is 5

- May appear artificially happy or always on a high

- Connects to higher ranks in life and associates with high society

- Highly intellectual, relates to complex information

- Relates to the present time, to the here and now

- Charming, handsome, and communicative

- Handy, creative, hardworking, and rewarding

- Spiritual and honest from within

- Relates to higher understanding

- Hopeful, faithful, and helpful

- Deals with multitasking and is good at it

- Unites people and places

I

---

its numeric value is 1

- All about "me, me, and me," and in fact, the "me" is the center of attention and relates to ego

- Great leader, charismatic, sweet, loved, and seeks love

- Active and always in action and motion

- Possesses some feminine traits

- Attracted to successful people and success in general

- Egocentric and is self-absorbed due to some hidden low self-esteem

- Compromises for love and glory

- Loves to be needed and helpful

J

---

its numeric value is 1

- Mainly happy and joyful

- Judgmental and purposeful

- Constantly in pursuit of union and balance

- Revolves around protection and is mainly protected

- Seeks and gets help in creating, changing, and achieving goals

- Represents leadership, success, and achievements

- Aspires to perfection and often reaches it

K

its numeric value is 1

- Always moves toward success, leadership, and being ahead
- Needs and seeks attention, love, and recognition, which may be the reason for its lack of balance
- A teacher and a great leader, yet needs to be more focused
- Often forgets that others have opinions and ideas that merit respect too
- Loud letter that looks for attention and gets it
- Knocks and shakes to get attention
- Needs and attracts changes constantly
- Is sensual, sexual, and sensational
- Relates more to the physical body than to the mind
- Charismatic, beautiful, and impulsive

L

***

its numeric number is 3

- Known for its ability to learn and teach

- Most of the time is loving, spiritual, and stubborn

- Has high or low moods, drive, and motivation

- Beautiful and relates to beauty

- Views oneself as superior even though the L may have some issues with self-esteem

- Always knows when change is required and acts upon it

- Curious about everything and anything

- Noisy, loud, and loves to express the self freely

- Connects and feels a part of everyone and everything

- Controller or a leader, unpredictable, and indecisive

- Up and down and all over the place with very little focus

- An excellent negotiator, especially in the material world

- Loving, sensitive, and always a great leader

- Loyal, loved, and supported by others

- Needs to be aware of the mood swings that come from seeking perfection and beauty

M

---

its numeric value is 4

- Matriarchal, feminine, sensitive, and fruitful

- Associates with and relates to motherhood, mothering, understanding, caring, and nurturing

- Has movement as a key word

- Able to move from one situation (or stage) to another easily

- Materialistic, yet balanced by spirituality

- Honest and devoted

- Always thinks and judges themselves and others

- True friend and lover, yet may look or feel cold or emotionally closed to others

- Looks for superiority, perfection, and high achievement

- Very sensitive, this can cause emotional ups and downs

- M is a feminine letter, and is therefore also sensitive

N

---

its numeric value is 5

- Extremely spiritual, represents the connection of body, mind, and soul as well as the connection between the earth and the sky
- Naturally communicates with all things as well as with different worlds
- Feminine, social, highly intuitive, competitive yet honest, supportive, and nurturing
- Loves new things, excitement, inventions, and movement
- Has mystery, magic, and mystique that makes it attractive
- Naturally possesses wisdom, insightfulness, and higher understanding
- Relates to life as eternal and spiritual, which may be what makes the N so beautiful and powerful
- Is communicative, creative, artistic, and mostly successful (if positive and spiritual)
- Is extremely social and needs to let go of the negativity that may sneaks in quietly

O

its numeric value is 7

- Holistic and spiritual

- Relates to soul development and has a high sense of purpose

- Enjoys and looks for peace

- Loves setting goals and reaching outstanding results

- Connects to people and things

- At times, compromises for peace, love, and unity

- Loving, caring, and always healing the self and others

- Complex and often therapeutic

- Relates to the angelic realms, psychology, philosophy, and energy

- Serves as a guide and a light for the self and others

- Finds joy and purpose from creating and being creative and productive

- Aspires to be someone important to others and the O achieves it

P

---

its numeric value is 8

- Relates to patriarchy (father figure) and protection

- Blessed, productive, creative, and fruitful

- Open to abundance and prosperity

- At times, appears to be closed, conservative, or traditional

- Looks for constant progress

- A leader at heart and an insightful teacher or mentor

- Makes an excellent partner and friend

- Quick to criticize

- Forgives and forgets easily

- Prefers to prioritize and follow through

Q

its numeric value is 1

- Curious and therefore questions and researches

- Mostly unstable and looks for stability

- Switches from liking something to disliking it and vice versa

- Uncertain and therefore questions choices, roles, and the future

- A wise leader and teacher

- Shifts constantly from being open to closed, positive to negative

- Has some self-esteem issues that may create blockages and inaction

R

---

its numeric value is 2

- Verbal and communicative yet must pay attention to keeping it positive and loving, avoiding negative communications or gossiping
- Loud, as it craves to be heard
- Competitive and desires to lead
- An excellent adviser, loves to express opinions and be helpful
- Prosperous and open to success
- Gain and profits oriented
- Can be manipulative and opinionated
- Soft, peaceful, and feminine, or strong and feisty

S

---

its numeric value is 3

- Relates to secrets and magic

- Insightful, wise, and knowledgeable

- Great advisor, storyteller, and innate teacher

- Successful, a doer, an achiever, and a winner

- Creative, peaceful, and positive

- Enjoys serving and helping others by being supportive

- Sensitive, external, sensual, and sexual

- Often relates to traveling, animals, nature, and open spaces

- Trusts easily and is trusted by people

- Must remember to avoid judging and to look beyond the surface

T

---

its numeric value is 4

- Relates to flights and heights

- Strives to soar to the top and achieves it easily

- Seeks to transform and improve everything and everyone

- Restless and is constantly seeking to get ahead

- Achieving balance between the spiritual and the physical is promoting the *T* even more

- Spiritual and faithful

- Tends to see a creative, positive future and creates excellent outcomes

- Dependable and lovable

- Beautiful inside and out

- Talented and loves to reinvent the self

- Benefits greatly from being calm and loving at all times and avoiding mood swings

- Tries new things that lead to learning and teaching

- Seeks to earn the best of the best, and therefore earns top dollars (pay) for whatever it does

U, V, and W

The numeric value is 6

- Relates to beauty, design, decoration, and fashion

- Excellent negotiator and knows how to connect and bond with others

- Possesses great social skills

- Always in a relationship or working on one

- Seeks perfection, harmony, and unity and enjoys it

- Romantic and has a strong desire to love

- Sees, feels, and lives with power without being restrained or constrained

- Possesses higher understanding and feels at one with all things

- Has the ability to unify and understand people naturally

X

---

its numeric value is 5

- Aspires to reach excellence at all times

- Both a skilled communicator and an entertainer

- Enjoys interacting with others

- Looks for beauty in everything and everyone

- Possesses extraordinary wisdom and the ability to understand complex matters and information

- Related to dualities and deals with several things at the same time

- Gets bored quickly

- Great mixer and is involved with many people and projects

- Often curious, loud, and noisy

- Attracts and loves commotion

Y

---

its numeric value is 1

- Great leader who stands on its own

- Loved by many

- Self-absorbed with some selfish traits

- Loves to be the first and last in everything as well as everywhere

- Stands out and loves attention

- Attractive and charismatic, but can have some jealousy issues

- Unique, individualistic, and independent

Z

---

its numeric value is 7

- Amazing, positive, and spiritual

- Finds it easy to love others

- Shares wise advices

- At times, compromises for peace and love

- Spiritual (especially focused on identity and purpose)

- Relates to growth and attracts recognition and compliments every step of the way

- Universal and unlimited

- Seeks a higher level of connections

- Conservative, traditional, and loves the status quo

Your Name Works for You!

Now that you have learned about the energy of each letter of your name—the ingredients of your soul—let us find out how the sum of your name, or the numerical code, gives us the accurate information regarding your actions, some of your abilities, and the way others view you.

To begin, add the numerical value of each letter of your first and last name. If you get a two-digit number as the sum, continue adding until you get a one-digit number. After you have calculated and determined the one digit number—your name code, which can be from 1 to 9—search in the following pages for the basic energy traits that relate to your code. That number represents you. It is your *numeric code* and contains specific information regarding the different aspects of your life in detail, including the way others most likely perceive you.

For example, I will use the name of my wonderful friend Esther Einstein.

E (5) + **S** (3) + **T** (4) +**H** (5) + **E** (5) + **R** (2) +**E** (5) + **I** (1) + **N** (5) + **S** (3) + **T** (4) + **E** (5) + **I** (1) + **N** (5) = 53.

Now, we are going to add 5 + 3 = 8 to attain a number.

Her numeric code is 8.

Let us begin with calculating the numeric codes of names.

The Letter	A	B	C	D	E	F	G	H	I	J	K	L
Numeric Value	1	2	3	4	5	8	3	5	1	1	1	3

The Letter	M	N	O	P	Q	R	S	T	U/V/W	X	Y	Z
Numeric Value	4	5	7	8	1	2	3	4	6	5	1	7

It is also important to know whether you were named after someone. If you were, then you might possess similar character traits, gifts, talents, and even a purpose that this person was known for. Therefore, it is beneficial to discover the history of the person you were named after.

As you can see, there are names and numbers everywhere!

We can calculate the names of restaurants, designers, artists, celebrities, pets, movies, objects, names of condominiums, boats, and much more.

When we calculate the energy of dates, we can calculate all dates: people and pets' birth dates, anniversaries, dates of holidays, days of the week, months, years, and so much more.

Also, we can calculate the energy of *things*, whether owned, rented, or borrowed: license plates/item/seat numbers (such as cars, boats, bicycles, airplanes, and more), home and business addresses, phone numbers, social security numbers, employee numbers, badge numbers, pet identification numbers, and even professional degrees and licenses.

A key concept here is *accepting* the universe just the way it is. The word accepting or acceptance in the Hebrew language is Kabbalah.

The study of Kabbalah teaches the process of seeing and accepting life exactly the way it is without trying to make it appear better. Only after you achieve acceptance can you achieve what you desire. Once you do, it will be easy for you to make wise decisions regarding your life, and if that is what you desire, improving on what you see or experience. In fact, knowing the laws of the universe and wisely applying it to work positively for you is powerful, rewarding, and actually good for the people you love and care for, so it is worth mastering.

Yes, to be in the right place at the right time is what makes us winners. In my opinion, this is real power! Applying the right universal law for the right situation is like having your personal lawyer work for you 24/7 preparing the right opportunities for you, making you act on the right ones, giving you the right solution or ideas, protecting you wherever you are, and guiding you to your desired success.

In the following pages, you will find the basic traits of these numeric codes of 1 to 9. Understanding the specific qualities and energies of each number will allow you to achieve your goals easily, rightfully, and safely.

Ready?

Let us get started!

Calculate, smile, and enjoy!

Your name Works for You

Name Number one

The number one is associated with and related to the sun and the zodiac sign, Leo. As such, the number one is competitive, ambitious, and strives to be number one at all times.

Desiring attention, love, power, and respect, it receives these qualities easily, as if by magic. Passionate about life, it always wants to lead. It seeks to be well known, appreciated, wanted, praised, glorified, recognized, and much more.

Number one is unique, creative, artistic, and charismatic. Furthermore, the one is romantic, protective, soft, and loving, but also mature and demanding at the same time. In fact, it represents a masculine father figure and is an excellent provider.

This number naturally receives the needed help to achieve any goal; therefore, success and leadership will be easier for this number. For number one, publicity and exposure are natural and expected. It shines just like the sun. Emotions of pride and ego need to be monitored and controlled, for it is a normal part of the number.

Number one is associated with some feelings of loneliness. Number one may experience those feelings personally or by whomever is related to it. In fact, it is recommended that number one is aware of this and make it a point to share with and include others more to make them feel adequate.

Name Number Two

———————◆·◆·◆———————

Number two relates to the moon and the zodiac sign, Cancer. In nature, the moon gains its energy from the sun. Similarly, number two may be dependent on others for their love, advice, and success. A two often deals with self-esteem issues or with self-validation, and therefore is overly sensitive and constantly seeking approval. A two is feminine, nurturing, sensitive (often oversensitive), sensual, passionate, rich with fantasy, and possesses great imagination.

In addition, it is highly intuitive and feels it in the stomach area. In fact, this number feels, knows, understands, and cares for others as a good mother would since it represents a feminine figure. It is hoped a two uses the intuition and the creative gifted abilities, for that will illuminate even more the magnificence of the self.

Two is family-oriented and may have issues related to select members of the family, especially that of a mother figure. The home represents the life and purpose of the two, and so is the need to take care of others.

It is recommended that this number speak up, protect, and stand up for the self, dispose of any guilt feelings, especially those related to the past, and boost the self-esteem and become independent. Finally, it is recommended to let go of the *need* to overprotect and smother others with love, advice, or help without being asked.

Name Number Three

Number three relates to Jupiter and to the zodiac sign, Sagittarius. The number three always looks positively toward the future and is mostly detached from the past. It possesses great vision and looks ahead with a positive and prosperous attitude.

Freedom, expansion, and open spaces are a vital part of the number and are extremely important. The expansion can be expressed and manifested in all areas of life: spiritual, material, intellectual, financial, or spatial.

An intuitive number, when a three follows its intuition, it is rewarded. Yes, it is known to be a winning number in all areas of life. It is safe to say that this number is secure and should take appropriate steps and chances to achieve its goals.

In other words, this number, thanks to its daring actions and trusting its great intuition with a positive attitude, attracts positive outcomes and success in all areas of life as well as financial fortune.

This number possesses a strong sense of justice. It often feels the need to protect, judge, or represent a person or the law in one form or another.

This number has difficulty committing (as it loves its freedom), focusing, and completing things until the end, as well as paying attention to details.

At times, a three may *seem* uncaring or even cold to others.

Name Number Four

Number four relates to Uranus and the zodiac sign, Aquarius. This number likes to be special, original, and innovative. Looking for unique solutions or ways to express itself, it has the ability to find solutions or ideas easily. Number four is a great inventor and improviser and relates to the new and modern. Often unpredictable, it relates to the unexpected. Letting go of the past is easy for number four. Furthermore, it lives guilt-free, carelessly, and without limits.

This number is associated with technology, electronic devices, and anything that has to do with the media, publicity, and TV. Number four is super intelligent and has high energy levels. It craves high social rank, large sums of money, and often seems like someone who has its head in the clouds.

The four is social, loving, and considered lovable by all. It needs and wants people, friends, and family, but loves and keeps its freedom and independence as a number one priority. It is a democratic number, which allows others to be and express themselves in a free and independent way.

Name Number Five

Number five relates to Mercury and the zodiac signs, Virgo and Gemini. Five relates to movement, positive attitude, beauty, spirituality, and materialism. It is always on the move, traveling, and restless. It also relates to modes of transportation. The number five enjoys being with others, communicating, and sharing from its vast pool of knowledge. Number five is communicative, creative, articulate, often of higher intellect, and possesses a great ability to comprehend complex information.

Most likely, a five is acting as a teacher since the achievements of the number are typically associated with its outstanding ability to comprehend complex information and to communicate it clearly to others.

Five is a thinker and a speaker and less of a doer. It can be a great actor, teacher, trader, singer, or anyone who uses the art of communication.

One of the great gifts of the five is its outstanding ability to understand the connection between the mind, body, and soul and communicate it to others in ways that is easily understood. Youthful, it always looks and feels younger. A five associates and feels more comfortable with those of the younger generation. It has a tendency to get bored easily and often handles multiple tasks all at once.

This number must avoid distractions, stay focused, complete all started projects, and avoid gossip and negative communication.

Name Number Six

Number six represents Venus and the zodiac signs Taurus and Libra. This number always relates to beauty, color, decorating, and looking great. It is also a number that relates to makeup, design, and art.

Harmony and beauty are very important to this number. There is more importance to outer beauty than inner beauty. A six cannot be alone and therefore attracts friends, relationships, and partnerships of different kinds.

Number six is romantic, passionate, and sexually oriented. It is a great negotiator and a listener who understands people and situations more than any other number.

It is a simple, yet strong and focused number that appreciates beauty and the material world. A six tends to attract material things.

It looks for peace and tranquility, and for that reason, gets along well with others. It feels connected to other people and enjoys participating in something bigger and stronger than itself.

The number six shows great hospitality traits that makes them wonderful entrepreneurs, hotel servers, and much more.

Name Number Seven

The number seven relates to Neptune and the zodiac sign, Pisces. Number seven is complex and represents the philosophical, mystical, psychological, and spiritual, and always relates to the development of the soul.

The seven puts caring, nurturing, healing, and guiding others as its first priority. This may at times create some feelings of sacrifice or compromise. In addition, it may be encumbered with strong emotional baggage. It has to let go of situations and emotions that are unlike love, especially if related to the past. It needs to get a grip on its feelings and prevent situations of self-destruction and avoidance with the possible need to escape reality through all kinds of addictions. Therefore, it is recommended for this number to monitor its habits and addictions.

Weakness and lack of energy is possible. Number seven has a deep need to be part of something or to belong to something big whether it is a group, a philosophy, or a person. It may have some identity issues internally.

It is a forgiving, loving soul that represents eternity. It would benefit greatly from a stronger sense of deserving and from practicing higher self-love. A seven can communicate clearly and easily. This number has a strong ability for healing and helping. This number has to remember to focus on living and enjoying the present moment free from the past.

Name Number Eight

Number eight relates to Saturn and the zodiac sign, Capricorn. Number eight means maturity (even at a young age), responsibility, determination, and drive. Careers, hierarchy, and management are very important to the eight, who pushes and reaches its goals by doing what it takes.

In fact, it is difficult for number eight to accept shortcuts. Extremely traditional, it may have an orthodox, religious side, with a need for a status and a name. The number desires fame, boundaries, and hierarchy, and tends to reach its goals. The number eight loves to be in control. Often it will find itself testing others as well as the self. Hard work for long periods is the life of an eight. The eight likes to do it all by itself without asking for help from anyone, even if it means long periods of hardship.

With difficulties to change circumstances, it accepts the situation as destiny, and in that sense, lives in harmony with the Creator. It is a number of development and building, yet forgetful of its interior. Realistically, an eight relates to *must* and *should do's*, tending to stress out when encountering authority.

It is always a profitable number or profit oriented. It will be even more successful if it takes care of the body, the mind, and the soul and not only of the tasks ahead.

Name Number Nine

The number nine often relates to Mars and to the zodiac sign, Aries. It represents strong physical energies, and we can see it in their need for leadership to be first in whatever they do. Nine is competitive, childish, independent, and often selfish.

A nine is an individualist and rebellious and dislikes hierarchy and authority. It has a strong passion for dancing and freedom of any kind, especially of self-expression and creativity. Nine is a young number. It is related to youth and feeling young, and in turn, attempts to act like one, doing whatever it wants in its own individualistic way without raising ethical issues. Aggressive and impulsive with lots of vitality, it acts like something within refuses to mature.

Its high energies are mainly in its head; therefore, a nine has to control its internal fights. A nine is very sensual and sexual. The number relates to medicine, therapy, healing, psychology, and the soul. A nine stands up for itself easily and successfully. It always takes the right actions that promote the self and the people they care about and love. It is easy for a nine to let go of anything or anyone that is not beneficial to him or her. It has deep-rooted opinions and insists on them.

They are great soldiers, lawyers, judges, therapists, dancers, musicians or healers, writers, philosophers, artists, accountants, business people, and bankers.

Part II

the Significance of Your Birth dates

The Significance Of Your Birth Date

———•◦•———

Does our birth date matter or influence our being?

Yes, it is part of our codes. When we are using awareness and consciously think, act, and speak with awareness, thereby manifesting what we desire, we rise above our nature positively. When I say awareness, I mean being aware of the way our body and soul automatically react under these energies. Thanks to the laws of attraction, we choose to act, react, speak, or think in ways that are rewarding and pleasing to us.

Let us look at the date of birth and learn about our wonderful self-attraction by understanding how the different dates translate into numbers and how those may influence us.

Here you identify the main traits, potentials, and gifts of each date.

I know you will enjoy and benefit greatly from calculating and discovering the main traits and the great potentials of your energy and those of the people you care for or those of the people you are in a relationship with.

Thanks to that same wisdom, you will be able to calculate and know the main energy traits of the year that you or your dear ones are currently in or the dates forthcoming.

I have noticed that it is also valid and true for birth dates of ideas, inventions, design, art, new business, and so much more.

The Birth Dates, Codes and Energy

The sum of the *day* of our birthday to a one-digit number teaches us about the way we choose to express ourselves as an individual and how others see us. We are inclined to express the rest of our numbers (from the birth date or our name) in the material world.

When the addition of two digits produces a two-digit number, add those two digits again until you get a single-digit number.

For example, a birth date of May 29, 1971, makes 29 the day of birth and 2 + 9 equals 11, a two-digit number. Add those two digits together, 1 + 1, equals 2. Therefore, 2 will be the **day** code number in this case.

After you have summed up the numbers to a one-digit number, go to the next page where you will read more about how you and others are most inclined to express the self and how you may appear to other people, unless you use awareness and choose differently.

I must make a point regarding the numbers 11 and 22. When we add those together to get one digit, we will get 2 and 4 (1 + 1 = 2 and 2 + 2 = 4). Yet, I want to remind you that those two combinations are considered special, spiritually high numbers, and powerful.

Go ahead and discover what your **day** of birth code is by summing it up to a one-digit number.

Decide whether you like how you are expressing yourself and the way others view you or not!

A powerful tool for creating change is through positive, corrective affirmations that will create new beliefs and will automatically improve the way you appear to others.

Some examples of general corrective affirmations for each number are included in the page that follows the one that describes the energy of each number. Simply write them down and keep them somewhere safe, or simply repeat the correction affirmation several times a day for twenty-one consecutive days. The results you will experience in both cases will be positively amazing.

Day Code #1

How do people with D1 tend to express themselves in the material world? How do they appear to others?

- A leader

- Powerful, ambitious, competitive, and loving yet also needy for love and attention

- Giving unlimited love and respect to people and often receiving the same in return

- Social and successful, though at times may seem lonely

- A well-known, respected, appreciated, wanted, praised, glorified, and recognized individual

- A one stands out in a crowd and will be seen as a unique, creative, artistic, charismatic, romantic, demanding, protective, mature leader

- Muscular and protective often seems to have fatherly (male) traits

- Seems to have and get all the right help needed to achieve any goal almost entirely by luck or by magic

- Shining like a star easily and naturally

- Always on a show

- Confident with a high self-esteem

Corrective Affirmations for
Day Code #1

———————

"I look like someone, and I am

- positive, guided, loved, helped, and supported;

- humble, regardless of my high position and power;

- enjoying many great and nurturing relationships with people;

- in great and positive relationships, based on love, respect, and higher levels of understanding, including with the younger people in my life;

- truly and honestly connected and part of people; and

- _____

  _____."

Day Code #2

How do people with D2 tend to express themselves in the material world? How do they appear to others?

- Dependent on others for their energy, love, support, and self-esteem

- Often will be viewed as overly nurturing, emotional, overprotective, or needy

- Sensual, passionate, rich with fantasy, and highly imaginative

- Highly intuitive, knows, feels, understands, and cares for others

- Family-oriented

- May seem to have some issues with certain members of the family, especially with a mother figure

- Attached to the past, resists changes, seems to have major problems letting go of the past

Corrective Affirmations for Day Code #2

"I look like someone, and I am

- powerful and independent and I have high self-esteem;

- looking at things in an objective way and am in control of my emotions;

- enjoying the outdoors, nature, and open spaces;

- I have wonderful, loving, caring, supporting, and nurturing relationships inside and outside the family circle;

- looking forward in life, detached from the past, and moving forward and toward the great and the new all the time;

- making wise choices especially regarding money and relationship matters;

- practicing good and healthy eating habits;

- in control about my body weight and shape; and

- _____

_____."

Day Code #3

———◆———

How do people with D3 tend to express themselves in the material world? How do they appear to others?

- Holding a big vision and looking ahead with a positive attitude

- Expanding in all areas of life—spiritual, materialistic, philosophical, traveling, or nomadic (freedom, expansion, and open spaces seem very important to the three)

- Daring, likes to take chances that leads it to advance and expand

- Intuitive and trusting its intuition

- A winner—rewarded and rewarding

- Someone with a strong sense of justice

- Needs or wants to protect or represent

- Have difficulties to commit

- May appear careless or emotionally cold toward others

- May seem to lack the focus needed to complete projects or pay sufficient attention to details

Corrective Affirmations for Day Code #3

"I look like someone, and I am

- decisive, focused, and committed;

- warm and loving;

- accountable to my commitments;

- seeing the big picture as well as all the details attached to it;

- a great listener who understands correctly what is being said and intended; and

- _____

  _____."

Day Code #4

How do people with D4 tend to express themselves in the material world? How do they appear to others?

- Special, original, innovative, looking for unique solutions or ways to express the self

- Able to easily find solutions or ideas

- A great inventor/improviser

- Strictly connected to the future and totally disconnected from the past (therefore separation or letting go of excess baggage from the past seems easy for the four)

- Without regret or guilt and that allows whatever is desired without thinking of ethical issues

- Related to technology, innovations, electronic devices, or anything that involves the media, publicity, TV, communications, and computers

- Related to heights, to flights, great visions, high social rank, and high energy levels

- This often makes the four look like it walks with its head in the clouds in need of being grounded

- Social and loved

- Needs to be surrounded by people and family, but wants to keep its freedom and independence above all

- Liberal, allows others to be free and independent

- Related to super intelligence in one way or another and is viewed as such

Corrective Affirmations for
Day Code #4

"I look like someone, and I am

- disciplined and who loves routine and commitments;

- enjoying living in the present moment and respect the past;

- caring, nurturing, grounded, balanced; and

- _____

_____."

Day Code #5

How people with D5 tend to express themselves in the material world? How do they appear to others?

- Related to movement, positive attitude, beauty, spirituality, as well as materialism
- Communicating with people and things, always sharing information and knowledge to the public and the media
- Articulate, possessing a great ability to comprehend complexity is a great teacher
- Much talk, little action (actor, teacher, trader, singer, etc.)
- Restless and always on the move
- Related to modes of transportation
- Knowledgeable, understanding the connection between mind, body, and soul
- Looking and feeling younger than his/her real age
- Associates and feels more comfortable with the younger generation
- Gets bored easily and jumps from task to task

Corrective Affirmations for Day Code #5

"I look like someone, and I am

- dynamic and flexible as well as determined and focused;

- physically active, positive, organized, peaceful, decisive, and a positive thinker;

- an excellent communicator who uses only clear, positive, creative communication (words);

- a talker and a great doer—I do what I say I will do; and

- _____

  _____."

Day Code #6

How people with D6 tend to express themselves in the material world? How do they appear to others?

- Related to beauty, color, decorating, and looking great, as harmony and beauty seem to be very important to the six

- It seems like the six gives more importance to outer beauty than inner beauty

- Related to partnerships and relationships of all kinds

- A great negotiator, listener, and an excellent trader

- Seems to understand each side in the relationship or partnership

- Simple and humble, yet strong and focused

- One who enjoys and appreciates material things, with the upside being that it looks like number six easily attracts them

- Someone who looks for peace and tranquility and seems to get along well with others

- Strongly connected with other people and enjoys participating in something bigger than the self and seems to be doing all this with love and harmony

- Romantic and sexually oriented and possesses a tremendous amount of passion

- A great designer, artist, and entrepreneur

Corrective Affirmations for Day Code #6

"I look like someone, and I am

- someone who cares about the soul and about what truly counts;

- beautiful inside and out;

- having true and good relationships with people; and

- _____

   _____."

Day Code #7

How do people with D7 tend to express themselves in the material world? How do they appear to others?

- Related to the abstract; philosophical, mysticism, psychology, and spirituality

- Has to do with the development of the soul one way or another (it seems the number seven puts high interest and value in caring, nurturing, healing, and guiding others)

- Someone who has powerful emotions

- Being in control of their emotions is beneficial and helps them to avoid situations of self-destruction, avoidance, and a deep need to escape through all kinds of addictions

- When they are doing or feeling good the way they like, they will have lots of energy

- Feel a need to be part of a spiritual community, something or someone bigger and important and at times may have issues that relate to identity

- A forgiving, loving soul that represents eternity

- Someone successful when practicing self-love

Corrective Affirmations for Day Code #7

"I look like someone, and I am

- someone who has high self-esteem all the time;

- balanced, decisive, focused, emotionally stable, and enjoy living in the present moment with a positive outlook for the future;

- confident in what I want;

- open to all good things and receive/achieve them easily;

- having a great and powerful memory, and I am using it well;

- in control (about feelings, situations) and always makes the best of every situation;

- independent, disciplined, profits oriented, and organized;

- energetic and physically in great shape;

- standing up for myself and dealing with situations and emotions wisely and immediately with ease; and

- _____
  _____."

Day Code #8

How do people with D8 tend to express themselves in the material world? How do they appear to others?

- Mature even at a young age
- Responsible, determined, possessing a powerful drive (careers and status seem to be extremely important)
- Pushing and reaching goals no matter what it takes
- Always in control and truly loving it
- Testing others and the self regularly without the ability to accept compromises — it's either black or white
- Extremely traditional and often religious
- Craving status and fame
- Striving to do and be the best at all times
- Engaging in hard work for prolonged periods
- Having issues with skin, bones, teeth, joints, and the back
- Constantly developing, working on something, building, preparing, cooking, remodeling, and more
- Enjoys doing all this alone without asking for help from anyone, even if it means long periods of hardships
- Has difficulties to change circumstances and stubbornly accept them as destiny, and in that sense, appears to be living in harmony with the Creator
- Cares less about his/her inner self and more about the outside (not introspective)
- Realistic
- It is all about musts, should dos, and hard work
- Who respects authority and would like to have it at all time
- Money and profits oriented

Corrective Affirmations for Day Code #8

"I look like someone, and I am

- flexible and dynamic and enjoy and accept other's helpful ideas and support;

- working well with others and delegating to others and achieves things easily;

- someone who knows and remembers to pay attention to the inner as well;

- enjoying new things; and

- _____

  _____."

Day Code #9

How do people with D9 tend to express themselves in the material world? How do they appear to others?

- Related to strong physical energies

- In the need for leadership and being first

- Independent, childish, and at times selfish as well as competitive

- Individualistic, rebellious, dislikes hierarchy, and authority

- Possesses a strong passion for dancing and freedom of any kind, especially of self-expression and creativity

- Looking and feeling younger and interacting with young people

- Doing whatever it wants without raising ethical considerations

- Aggressive and impulsive with lots of vitality, almost like something within refuses to mature

- Having strong energies, mainly in the head

- Needs to be more in control of internal conflicts

- Sensual and sexual

- Related to medicine, therapy, healing, psychology, and the soul

- Opinionated and inflexible

- Impulsive and has strong urges

- In survival mode, always at war

- Who easily ends or lets go of anything that is old, negative, or unhealthy, rightfully and easily

Corrective Affirmations for
Day Code #9

———◆◆◆———

"I look like someone, and I am

- seeing the entire picture with all its details, options, and opportunities;

- decisive and at peace;

- someone who truly cares about others' opinions, thoughts, and feelings, enjoying life and is at peace with the world and others in it, just the way they are; and

- _____

  _____."

the Birth month Code

The Month Codes

You may already be familiar with the signs of the zodiac.

Each zodiacal sign relates to a number. That number is also a code that reveals the way we think, feel, and act, unless we are in a higher awareness and choose differently.

In this section, I am sharing with you the main energy traits of each zodiac sign and its related number.

As a reminder, here are the dates corresponding to each sign:

March 21 to April 19 — Aries

April 20 to May 20 — Taurus

May 21 to June 20 — Gemini

June 21 to July 22 — Cancer

July 23 to August 22 — Leo

August 23 to September 22 — Virgo

September 23 to October 22 — Libra

October 23 to November 21 — Scorpio

November 22 to December 21 — Sagittarius

December 22 to January 19 — Capricorn

January 20 to February 18 — Aquarius

February 19 to March 20 — Pisces

Read and enjoy!

Aries (9)

Related to the planet Mars and number nine. Strong physical energies that may be concentrated in the head of the Aries.

- Always ready to take the right action
- Desires to be in the lead, recognized, praised, and famous as well as number one at whatever he/she does
- Pushes forward in life with great courage and determination
- Looks for a breakthrough wherever possible
- Individualist who dislikes hierarchy or authority while enjoying authority over others
- Often looks for respect and attention from others and things
- Competitive
- Always desires to look good and be successful in front of others, especially in front of the self
- Values freedom of expression
- Possesses great passion for dancing, music, art, and any other form of self-expression
- Values freedom of expression
- Fast to react, judge, and criticize but cannot stand to be criticized
- Always tries to look good in the eyes of others and wants to appear as goody-goody
- Often looks younger than his/her age
- Aggressive and impulsive with lots of vitality
- At times childish, almost like something within the self refuses to mature
- Enjoys working and dealing with all that is related to youth

- Positive and optimistic and has the natural ability to overcome any situation

- Always starts or works on new projects, but rarely completes them

- Possesses a strong desire for material objects

- Easily takes the things desired without ethics issues

- Deals with internal conflicts, anger, aggression, and negative thoughts, and this may cause strong and frequent headaches or loss of energy

Taurus (6)

Related to Venus and to the number six. Movement, positivity, communications, peace, pleasure, and looking good and young.

- Represents balance between the material and the spiritual and looks for a pleasurable, comfortable, and peaceful living

- Nurturing and loving

- Desires to better the self and earns it

- Has the ability to see positive outcomes and rewards in people, places, and situations

- Restless and always moving forward in life

- Great communicator who enjoys teaching others the wisdoms acquired and earned

- Articulate

- Has a great ability to comprehend complex concepts

- Highly intuitive, has extrasensory perceptions and abilities

- Understands the connection between mind, body, and soul

- Always relates to the secrets and wisdoms of life

- Easily connected to this universe as well as to other dimensions and people; sees and feels it

- Great student

- Invests time in his/her life researching and investigating everything around and looks for ways to improve the surrounding environment

- Independent and productive

- Seeks freedom and space to express her/his self

- Mostly looking and feeling good, dynamic, and young

- Easily feels comfortable with those of a younger generation
- Gets bored easily and handles several things at the same time
- Has the gift of handling material and spiritual things at the same time and with excellent balance
- Must watch out for distractions, stay focused, and complete all started projects
- Loving
- Has a high emotional intelligence
- Attracts abundance of love, warmth, and wealth rightfully and easily and gives back in abundance
- Honest and expects others to be honest in their affairs
- Often prefers maintaining the peace, the comfort, or the status quo and may push away or reject the people, situations, or things that threaten
- Would benefit greatly from standing up for him/her self and to express his/her wants and needs clearly
- If suppressed, this negative energy may affect the throat area or manifest excess weight

Gemini (5)

Related to Mercury and to the number five. Related to beauty, colors, decorating, multitasking, trading, and looking great.

- Has seemingly contradicting characteristics, but manages to keep a natural balance between them
- Pays more attention to the way things look than to their essence
- May be viewed or considered superficial by others
- Deals with opposites and contrasts easily and naturally as if they complemented each other
- Great communicator, negotiator, and listener
- Has the ability to persuade, entertain, and understand others
- Good at business and trading or anything that requires negotiating skills
- Dynamic, active, and productive
- Persistent in reaching his/her goals
- Honesty is extremely important to Gemini for its serenity, peace, and harmony
- Gets along well with others
- Finds meaning in closeness with others
- Loves to participate in something bigger than itself
- Loves to be unique
- Often deals with issues regarding its personality and its self-identity (doubting its place and purpose)
- Has a hard time looking within to view the self in an objective way
- Has difficulty with humility
- Curious, creative, romantic, passionate, and sensual

- Relates to music, art, and painting

- Possesses a great imagination

- Craves respect (This is extremely important to the Gemini who knows how to easily give it and get it.)

- Would benefit from keeping focused on important things and completing all open projects before initiating new ones

- Needs to be more decisive and clear in his/her actions since indecisiveness may affect the hands, arms, shoulders, and body coordination

Cancer (2)

Related to the moon and to the number two. Creative, sensitive, intuitive, sensual, nurturing, protective and manipulative.

- Tends to be dependent on others for their energy, love, advice, self-esteem, and sense of self
- Possesses a strong desire to live and give life
- Extremely creative
- Craves a safe environment for itself and for the people it cares for
- Often viewed as overprotective
- Views the present or the future through lenses of the past
- Has the ability to rise and fall as if nothing happened, to look beyond, and therefore achieves great changes for the self and others
- Has a great ability to understand, nurture, and care for loved ones
- Often smothering and codependent
- Feminine, sensual, and physical
- Needs to feel loved and gives love easily
- Finds great joy and purpose in helping others
- Needs to be reassured
- Restless and creative
- Jumps from one project to another, from one goal to another, and always moves forward in life
- Wise, knowledgeable, and realistic
- Craves attention
- Desires to be and feels important to others
- Often known for its fertile imagination, sensitivity, and strong intuition

- Feelings are strongly felt in the stomach

- Its oversensitivity tends to create issues and dramas, often associated with the mother figure

- At times, carries a deep sadness and a strong desire to escape or hide

- Can be jealous and envious, both are a consequence of its oversensitivity

- Needs to learn to let go of experiences from the past, to boost its self-esteem, to become independent, and to beware of its constant mood changes

- Cancer would benefit greatly if it learns to light its own light before it turns to heal, care, and nurture others

- It has to learn to trust its intuition, to relax and enjoy life openly without guilt trips; otherwise, it may affect the stomach, the digestive system, or the chest area.

Leo (1)

Related to the sun and to the number one. Leadership, charming, caring, realistic and practical.

- Mature, responsible, determined, and related to status conscious

- Charming and charismatic, loves people, and seeks love and respect

- An excellent friend to have

- Tends to have big groups of friends sometimes only for very short periods

- Desires to lead

- Constantly testing others that can cause pain, misunderstanding, and drama (This can lead to separation from others that causes even more drama and pain.)

- Has a strong drive to help others and to win their love, respect, and praise (This tends to create unbalanced or unstable relationships.)

- Realistic and practical

- Directive, it's all about should and must dos as well as hard work

- Wants to be on stage or the center of attention, and he/she is likely to get it without asking for anyone's help

- A great listener

- Known for understanding others well and not only through spoken words

- A great developer and builder who enjoys doing it all alone and could benefit greatly from delegating the right things to others to make life easier

- Motivated by material gain and the status it brings

- Attaches more attention to his/her appearance than to other people's feelings

- Usually warm and loving, but can also be cold and uncaring

- Would benefit greatly from paying closer attention to the people he/she are in a relationship with and to their own life structure, support, and love

- Otherwise, it may manifest in the Leo's body, especially in the heart, the back, the teeth, and the skin

Virgo (5)

Related to Mercury and to the number five. Creative, practical, organized, childish, sexual, judgmental and rebellious.

- Critical, judgmental, aggressive, and discriminative
- Desires to be in the lead, to be first in whatever project he/she is involved
- Competitive, childish, and often independent as well as selfish
- Known to be highly creative, effective, organized, and practical
- Has the ability to distinguish between right and wrong and the needed and wanted from the unneeded
- Known to be a clean freak
- Individualistic and rebellious, and dislikes any form of hierarchy and authority
- Passionate about dancing and freedom of any kind, especially that of self-expression and creativity
- Young at heart and easily relates to youth
- Feels young and attempts to act young, not paying attention to any ethical issues that may raise
- Possesses strong energies that are mainly in the head
- Must control its internal conflicts
- Aggressive and impulsive with lots of vitality
- Extremely sensual and physical
- Intellectual, critical, and often involved with medicine, therapy, healing, psychology, and the soul
- Idealist and has strong internal conflicts mostly about justice
- Has deeply rooted opinions and is stubborn about them

- Virgo would benefit from monitoring its strong urges and impulses, slow down, and listen more.

- All about survival

- Often looks at things as a matter of life or death, which may affect the health of the Virgo's digestive system

Libra (6)

Related to Venus and to the number six. Artistic, creative and attractive.

- Sensitive — looks for excitement in everything and everyone

- Values friendships while measures everything up to the smallest detail

- Optimistic and always looks for the good in people and in everyone

- Has great ideas

- Continuously searches for ways to achieve all goals easily and safely

- Relates to beauty, design, makeup, colors, art, and all that affects his/her appearance

- Active and creative

- Enjoys doing and organizing things for itself and others

- Desires to be special and unique

- Good advisor, which gives him/her a sense of importance and power

- Good negotiator

- Has the ability to understand people's needs

- Virgo's profound understanding of people can cause over involvement

- Can feel very lonely and misunderstood

- Responsible soul and acts like one at all times

- Cares and helps others, but must remember to take care of the self as well

- There is internal conflict between deep involvement with helping people and letting go, and this creates great stress and guilt feelings that may affect Libra's metabolism

Scorpio (2)

Related to Pluto and to the number two. Sensitive, intuitive, sensual, sexual and a fighter.

- Dependent on others' love and affection even if the Scorpio appears to be strong and independent

- Often oversensitive and keeps it all inside

- A fighter. Needs to win every game/time/one/thing.

- Looks at failure as a reason to succeed and will use it as a jumping board for he/she comes out often stronger than before

- Uses pain as a reason to succeed and comes out even stronger than before

- Feels and understands people deeply even though he/she may not appear like this at first

- Dominated by its feelings and emotions, which generates even more feelings and emotions

- Extremely romantic, sensual, and physical

- Impulsive and aggressive

- Looks to the past with difficulties to let go and often has an issue with a motherhood figure at a young age

- Forgives and forgets easily, and this great ability is what allows the fabulous Scorpio to move fast in life

- Looks for gain and success in every situation

- Enjoys healing theories, psychology, and any knowledge that can benefit them one way or another

- Enjoys looking good and unique in the eyes of others and within him or her self

- Creative and a builder and often ends things and starts new ones as if nothing happened

- Building and destroying provides a great sense of emotional excitement for the Scorpio

- Recognizes real power, admires it, and connects to it with ease

- Follows only people who have real power, otherwise will rebel

- Loves things that come easily, especially gifts

- Loves to be pampered and catered to especially if it relates to fun, the body, the senses, and emotions

- Charming and knows how to use its charm and magic and pulls it often in a manipulative way

- Scorpio is feminine, sensual, and sexual, nurturing (represents motherhood), affectionate, and often oversensitive (This may affect their sexual or reproduction organs and at times their memory.)

Sagittarius (3)

Related to Jupiter and to the number three. Communicator, outgoing, positive, honest and assertive.

- Represents and relates to expansion in all areas of life
- An excellent communicator who is outgoing, friendly, and a great friend to have
- Enjoys expressing himself or herself freely, especially personal opinions
- Often viewed as bold and rude since Sagittarius tends to say whatever they think in a direct way and without filters
- Warm, loving, and caring, and prepared to fight for what is fair
- Honest and expects honesty in return
- Dynamic and enjoys moving fast through situations especially when it sees the need to interfere for what is right
- Portrays a great image of being knowledgeable in all areas of life
- Often enjoys sharing and teaching their personal wisdom and knowledge to others
- Assertive and direct, as well as energetic and active
- Possesses a great ability to deal with several things at the same time
- Tends to lose focus easily; must remember to stay focused and complete all started tasks and goals
- Sees the big picture and must learn to pay attention to the details
- Is loving and lovable and is always seeking love
- Often may appear distant and cold to others
- Judgmental and looks for justice within everything and everyone (This may create issues with his or her legs and knees as well as with the digestive system.)

Capricorn (8)

Related to Saturn and to the number eight. Competitive, career oriented, mature, materialistic and conservative.

- Mature, responsible, and often extremely serious
- Career, goal setting and success are very important to them
- Aspires to reach higher levels of success in society
- Looks at successful and powerful people with admiration; seeks their company, their love, their respect, and is often envious of powerful and successful people
- Works hard to copy successful people and tries to reach similar success
- Competitive and will do whatever needs to be done in order to reach certain heights
- Equates material things with success, for they are his/her main goals
- Traditionally conservative and highly religious
- Extremely serious about life and reality
- Relates to life as black or white
- Has high expectations for themselves and others
- Constantly judging other people based on their status
- Is often angry and holds a strong feeling of missing out on things in life
- Lives to achieve a certain name and reputation even if it entails long and hard working hours
- Must learn to schedule some fun time besides work, work, work
- Looks for stimulations of all kinds, but still wants to be in control
- An excellent taker, but has to learn to be a better giver
- Feels the constant need to control others and this may cause issues with teeth, bones, skeleton, and liver, and at times, also panic attacks

Aquarius (4)

Related to Uranus and to the number four. Active, creative, modern, and innovative.

- Loves to be special, original, and innovative
- Views the past in a unique way and constantly looks to improve it
- Related to all that is new and modern and loves using new technologies and devices
- Seeks to reach higher levels of success (in the material and the spiritual world) no matter what
- Extremely loving, lovable, loyal, honest, and is a great friend to have
- Active, creative, and overflowing with ideas
- Looks for brand new ideas to reinvent themselves and others
- Possesses a deep desire to influence and improve society
- Enjoys food, especially gourmet dishes
- Known to be intellectual, wise, and knowledgeable
- Appreciates traditions and customs, family and friends
- Has difficulties committing; prefers to stay free and independent
- Looks for freedom, especially that of self-expression
- Mainly humble and loving, yet possesses a strong sense of pride, which can lead to internal conflicts
- Rebellious and seeks to be in control wherever possible
- Strong and powerful when it knows the right direction to take
- Must remember to live life without conflicts or doubts and to be decisive because this can create physical issues that will manifest in coordination and the Aquarius legs

Pisces (7)

Related to Neptune and to the number seven. Caring, loving, spiritual, philosophical and individualistic.

- Is drawn to complexity: philosophical, mystical, psychological, and spiritual domains

- Loves open spaces and nature

- Enjoys matters related to the soul and its development

- Experiences extremes such as highs and lows, poverty and wealth, weight changes, etcetera

- Often seems to be individualistic, yet part of the whole one

- Works well with other independent individuals in total balance and treats them as equals

- Enjoys caring, nurturing, healing, and guiding others

- Focuses mostly on other people's needs and forgets about his/her needs, which may lead to feelings of compromising, sacrifice, or being taken advantage of

- Often suppresses his/her emotions in order to feel safe and protected

- Has trouble letting go and often holds old baggage from the past for long periods

- Loves music, and it helps the Pisces to rejoice and let go of negative feelings; otherwise, it may turn inward and create situations of self-destruction

- May look to escape from heavy, emotional feelings through other habits or addictions

- An excellent communicator and uses it wisely

- Looks for relaxation and pleasure in any situation

- Reinvents life, the self, and situations, and is able to change instantaneously even though it resists change
- Pisces suffers at times from lack of energy
- May have issues with their feet and the lymphatic system

purpose/destin Y   Code

Our Purpose/Destiny Code

The sum of our birth date numbers is important for two reasons. First, it reveals some of the main traits of our purpose in life. Second, it reveals the quality of our relationship with another person in our life. This person may be a family member, friend, life partner, business partner etc.

I have a feeling you are going to love this part, so go ahead calculate and enjoy!

The sum of our entire birth date is the sum of all the digits in a person's birth date. For example, April 27, 1963, with April being the fourth month will equal:

$4 + 2 + 7 + 1 + 9 + 6 + 3 = 32$

Now we add the 3 to the 2—since it is a two-digit number—and we get 5.

First, that number gives us some important information—main energy traits about the *destiny number* or *purpose number*, as most people prefer.

In fact, it will provide a clear indication about our *main purpose* traits in life, our gifts, and some indication as to the corrections—what we came here to do and experience.

Second, destiny numbers can help us know in advance some of the main traits of any given relationship. In the pages that follow the destiny numbers, we are going to look at the *relationship numbers*. We get that number by adding one's destiny number to that of the person of interest. The relationship number helps us to understand the main traits, quality, base, and type of the relationship.

Let us first address the destiny numbers.

The basic traits of destiny number one is

- To lead and be in the lead

- To do big things and to influence others

- To attract lots of attention

- To produce and create in a unique way

- To protect and guide, but mainly to be well known

- To be a great manager, advisor, teacher, movie star, excellent banker, or athlete

- To be a great starter of projects

- To be a great giver and an excellent provider

- To be desired, charismatic, loved, and loving

- To constantly self-improve and become self-motivated

- To have high levels of self-esteem and an unlimited supply of help from the universe

- To deal with young children within or outside his/her family

- To deal with ego issues and some loneliness feelings

- They are great managers, babysitters, leaders, investors, teachers, and well-known people

The basic traits of destiny number two is

- To revolve around the home and the family, nurturing, guiding, and loving
- To be oversensitive, intuitive, and wise
- To be great in receiving from others and life
- To receive easily whatever they want
- To be loved, cared for, appreciated, supported, protected and provided
- To be great advisors, teachers, and leaders since people follow them and their charismatic personality
- To be productive and creative and to use their love and talents to their benefit and that of the people they love
- To be blessed, fertile, productive, and open to prosper and success
- To be attractive, sensual, and sexual
- To posses high self-esteem from the people in their lives and their surroundings
- To focus on the past
- Would benefit from being outgoing, independent, responsible with money, confidante, and self-sufficient
- Would benefit from being in control of their emotions, their weight, and their money
- To be excellent chefs, healers, caregivers, babysitters, artists, and writers

The basic traits of destiny number three is

- To expand in one or more (or all) areas of life—the spiritual, material, and intellectual
- To live as a nomad and move from place to place
- To travel a lot and have longings to distant places, people or feelings
- To advance and grow in life by taking chances and winning
- To protect, represent, and judge
- To expand and to express its feelings without filters or boundaries
- To spend most of their life outdoors enjoying nature and interacting with animals
- To love its freedom, has difficulties to commit or to complete open projects
- To be lucky in all undertaking if taking the right actions/chances
- To be excellent Realtors, gardeners, animal trainers, deliverers, lawyers, salespeople, and judges as well as gamblers

The basic traits of destiny number four is

- To be the agent of changes on a local scale or on a worldwide one

- To invent the right and needed solutions for the self and others

- To not be bound by the past

- To be open to innovations, technology, and communication

- To relate to heights: physical, spiritual, and status related

- To love tasting and living life in a unique way, guilt free

- To act often as if it is allowed and deserves everything, and to go and get it without asking any questions

- To aspire to reach high levels of success

- To be positive and to have a positive outlook about life and people

- To love its freedom and independence and to have difficulties to commit

- To be excellent inventors, technicians, flight attendants, pilots, and media people

The basic traits of destiny number five is

- To absorb complex information and to communicate it to others

- To have great communication skills

- To instruct, guide, teach, sales, and entertaining

- To be restless and to deal with vehicles and other modes of transportation

- To be firmly rooted in the material world, and to always want more

- To deal with several things all at the same time with a great ability and sense of control

- To communicate with everyone and everything including the souls and other worlds

- To have the urge to perform, entertain, and be the center of attention

- To be among the great actors, singers, teachers, speakers, salespeople, and lawyers

The basic traits of destiny number six is

- To be evolved around beauty, color, makeup, aesthetics, decoration, and the way things look from the outside
- To deal with, solve, work with, and attract all kinds of relationships and partnerships, mainly romantic ones
- To be a skilled negotiator; has a gift for balanced give and take
- To pay attention to the way things and people look and will always present itself in a beautiful light
- To look good and to act with diplomacy
- To enjoy entertaining, parties, friends, and good food
- To learn to be more independent, especially emotionally
- To look inside, discovering or knowing the self, and hopefully take corrective actions
- To be destined to be excellent designers, artists, writers, entrepreneurs, salespeople, and hoteliers

The basic traits of destiny number seven is

- To revolve around spirituality, philosophy, the mystical, and psychology

- To deal with the development of the self and the soul

- To care, nurture, heal, and guide others in their own journey

- To be complex, complete, and loving

- To have issues with the self since it is often destined to lack balance between giving and taking

- To have great energies that will most likely be used to make major karmic corrections accumulated from previous lifetimes

- To feel at times that others take advantage of it, taking more than they give

- To seek peace at every cost

- It could feel being used, underestimated, taking advantage of, being underpaid, separated, or compromising

- Would benefit greatly from communicating clearly its needs, trusting, opening up, enjoying life, being present, and eliminating the need to escape from their feelings or from their reality

- To be excellent philosophers, doctors, spiritual healers, writers, and counselors

The basic traits of destiny number eight is

- To lead and advance in life and career

- To be rooted and related to the material world

- To manage with determination and drive and to collect rich rewards from it

- To be spiritually and physically balanced

- To be traditional or conservative

- To crave and reach the status and fame desired

- To be realistic, hard working, and achieve financial success

- To be excellent hoteliers, restorers, both managers and workers, business owners, preachers, and teachers

The basic traits of destiny number nine is

- To be good at starting new projects

- To let go, release, or end old or limiting projects, relationships, and situations that are no longer useful

- To rebel and compete, which could be interpreted as childish and aggressive

- To be impulsive, energetic, and have lots of vitality

- To express itself mainly through music or dancing

- To be extremely sensual, physical, and sexual

- To focus on the smallest details and less on the big picture

- To act like a warrior and fight if necessary to defend its point of view

- To be involved with all that is related to medicine, therapy, healing, psychology, and the soul

- To be destined to be excellent warriors, lovers, therapists, doctors, surgeons, accountants, dancers, investors, writers, and judges

relationships BY the numBer

Relationships by the Number

The second important information we can get from the destiny number (the one-digit sum of the entire birth date) is the quality and base of the relationship we have or will have with each person in our life.

What great power we can find in knowing whom we are and what we came here to do! Even more so, think about the power you acquire by knowing the destiny number of your loved ones, friends, and work colleagues.

In fact, from their destiny number we can learn about their energy. Who are they? What are their likes and dislikes? Even better, we can discover the traits and quality of our relationship with them. This can always be beneficial to know in any relationship.

Yes, adding your destiny number — the sum of all the digits of the entire birth date expressed as a one-digit number, to that of the person you are in a relationship with — will give you a new number (remember to sum it to a one-digit number also). That number is called the *relationship number*.

The relationship (code) number reveals the main traits, type, quality, and energy of the relationship. This can help in stimulating, motivating, or improving the relationship and avoiding disappointments or false expectations.

Calculate and find out for yourself. I have a feeling it is going to be beneficial to you!

Basic Traits of Relationship Number One (R1)

- The relationship is ambitious and competitive with a strong desire to be in control and to be loved — any type of love.

- This relationship wants to be number one, be famous, respected, appreciated, wanted, and praised.

- This relationship is unique, creative, artistic, and charismatic.

- R1 loves the attention and the support that it is often giving and receiving.

- It is mature and masculine, much like a father figure.

- It is mature and independent, but also loving and romantic.

- R1 always receives the help needed to achieve any goal, almost as if it has massive amounts of luck.

- The relationship gets lots of publicity and exposure. It seems to shine like the sun — naturally.

- R1 may have some ego and pride issues. They need to monitor and control these emotions.

- They are socially active even though at times they carry feelings of loneliness.

- This relationship would benefit from sharing more with others and allowing them into their environment.

- They will often deal with the younger generation.

Basic Traits of Relationship Number Two (R2)

- It is a family-oriented relationship. It may have issues with some family members, especially with a mother figure.

- The relationship is nurturing, sensitive, and attached to the past while stubbornly resisting change.

- R2 is characterized by dependency on each other and on the outside (love, stability, money, etc.) and can be easily influenced.

- This relationship is sensual, passionate, and rich with fantasies and imagination.

- R2 is highly intuitive; it knows, feels, understands, and cares for others.

- This relationship tends to reassure itself through food and spending binges.

- R2 is creative and productive.

- This relationship will benefit from a boost in self-esteem.

- It also needs to be self-motivated without relying on outside stimuli.

- The relationship's life has a need to take care of others. Remember to take care of the relationship first without guilt trips or feelings of selfishness.

- R2 often has to learn to let go of the past with its baggage, enjoy the present, and have confidence in the future.

- It also has to get out more, travel, and enjoy nature.

Basic Traits of Relationship Number Three (R3)

- An R3 holds a bigger vision for the future and looks ahead with a more positive attitude.

- Freedom, expansion, and open spaces are very important to the relationship.

- This relationship is all about expansion in all areas of life: spiritual, material, and philosophical, and in space and knowledge.

- It is mostly traveling and moving. In fact, this relationship is positive and together, and they would gamble or take the right chances to advance and expand even more.

- Highly intuitive, this relationship should follow and trust its intuition, for it is a highly rewarding and winning relationship. This relationship attracts good luck and other rewards (material and spiritual).

- This relationship has a strong sense of justice. It feels the need to protect or represent someone or the law. It often stands up for what is right.

- This relationship has issues and difficulties when it comes to commitments (for it loves its freedom), or to stay focused and complete projects until the end while paying attention to the details.

- Partners in a number three relationship may seem cold or careless to others. Therefore, they need to show more love, attention, and affection since it is needed and wanted by others and their partners too (even though at times, the partners seem to not need or want it).

Basic Traits of Relationship Number Four (R4)

- An R4 is special, original, innovative, and looking into the future for unique solutions or ways to express itself in an individualistic way.

- It likes to stand out and be different and unique, which it most likely is. In fact, this relationship has the ability to invent or find solutions and ideas easily.

- This relationship is known for its great improvising character or ability. Unexpected and unpredictable, this relationship has a strong feeling of deserving. They want to taste and to try things without raising ethical or guilt issues. Together they are allowed everything.

- They are strictly connected to the future and totally disconnected from the past. In fact, separating or letting go of excess baggage is easy for this relationship.

- The relationship has very little regrets or guilt.

- This relationship relates to technology, innovations, electronic devices, or anything that has to do with the media, publicity, TV, communications, and computers.

- This relationship relates to heights, therefore to flights, great visions, high social ranks, and high energy levels. At times, it seems as if the partners in the relationship are high or walking with their heads in the clouds. Therefore, it is required that the partners pay attention and be more grounded.

- This relationship is extremely social and loved by others.

121

- This relationship needs and wants to attract people and family, yet loves and maintains its freedom and independence as a number-one priority.

- The relationship is based on democratic values, freedom, and independence.

- It is also based mainly on higher intellect, intelligence, and values.

Basic Traits of Relationship Number Five (R5)

- R5 is all about communications. In fact, this relationship is constantly communicating between themselves, to the media, and to other people by telephone, fax, letters, words, actions, body language, and so on.

- For this relationship, publicity and exposure are easy and natural.

- This relationship always sees and thinks positively. Keeping their communications positive is the real key to their success.

- This relationship has an internal beauty that shines naturally, which may contribute by the spiritual level of this union or partnership.

- The bases of this relationship are the synergy of higher intellect, wisdom, and spirituality, and this is in complete balance with a practical, strong, materialistic connection and attraction.

- It is articulate and possesses a great ability to comprehend complex information. Its achievements are typically associated with this skill to comprehend and communicate clearly.

- It must work on the tendency of the relationship to speak more and do less.

- Socially active, it seems like this relationship is popular

- An R5 is restless and always on the move, traveling, taking action, changing careers/fields, and constantly evolving in life. They give much attention to the various modes of transportation.

- This relationship looks and feels younger and often associates with and feels more comfortable with those of the younger generation.

- Gets bored easily that is why they multitask.

- The relationship handles multiple activities at the same time and must remember to complete all current projects before starting a new one.

- The relationship benefits greatly from avoiding gossip and negative communications, as positive communication is vital to their success.

Basic Traits of Relationship Number Six (R6)

- Beauty, color, looks, and harmony are very important to the relationship.

- Essential inner qualities are less important than appearances.

- An R6 is obsessed with relationships (terms and conditions) of their own and of others.

- They are constantly negotiating and finding good, creative solutions for everyone involved.

- Six is a simple, yet strong and focused relationship.

- Focused on the material world and will easily attract material success.

- An R6 is social, outgoing, and loving.

- It constantly looks for peace and tranquility and gets along well with others.

- Feels connected to other people and has a yearning to participate in building together with others something bigger and stronger than they are.

- They are often romantic, passionate, and sensual.

Basic Traits of Relationship Number Seven (R7)

- Philosophical, mystical, psychological, and spiritual, an R7 is all about the development of the soul.

- Often involved with caring, nurturing, healing, and guiding others, yet may harbor feelings of sacrifice or compromise (emotionally closing off their feelings).

- May carry heavy emotional issues and has to learn to let go of those feelings, situations, and relationships that are less beneficial to them.

- This strong relationship must get a grip on their feelings; otherwise, this powerful energy can turn inward, and we can find situations of self-destruction, avoidance, and a deep need to escape using drugs and alcohol.

- It should also be aware and monitor habits and addictions.

- Weakness and lack of energy are possible.

- It can have identity issues internally. The relationship has a deep need to be part of something or to belong to something, whether it is a group, a philosophy, or a person.

- It harbors feelings of sacrifice and may even be missing out on things such as business opportunities.

- An R7 is a forgiving and loving relationship that represents eternity.

- The partners must use a stronger sense of deserving and practice more self-love.

- This relationship has a strong ability for healing and helping, yet one must remember to do so when asked, and try to keep himself/herself happy and safe.

- It can communicate clearly and easily.

- It focuses on living and enjoying the present moment.

Basic Traits of Relationship Number Eight (R8)

- It relates to maturity (even at a young age), responsibility, determination, and drive.

- Career and management are very important to the relationship; they push to reach their goals no matter what it takes.

- It loves to be in control.

- It constantly tests others and the relationship itself without the ability to accept shortcuts. It is either black or white and is very traditional.

- There is a basic, maybe orthodox, religious side to this relationship.

- The relationship has a need for a well-known status and name.

- The partners in the relationship desire fame, boundaries, and hierarchy. Therefore, working hard for long periods are the life of the eight couple, who often enjoy doing tasks without asking for help. They are realistic, focused on musts and should dos, and stress out regarding authority.

- It has difficulties changing circumstances, so it accepts it as destiny, and in that sense, lives in harmony with the Creator.

- It is always a profit-oriented relationship or together, attracts profits easily.

- It is a relationship that enjoys developing and building, yet forgetful of its interior, and that may cause issues with skin, bones, teeth, joints, and the back.

Basic Traits of Relationship Number Nine (R9)

- An R9 is represented by strong physical energies.

- It has a need for leadership, to be first in what it does.

- The relationship is very competitive, childish, and somewhat selfish as well as independent.

- The partners in the relationship are often individualistic and rebellious who dislike hierarchy and authority.

- The couple possesses a strong passion for dancing and freedom of expression of any kind, especially of self-expression and creativity.

- The relationship relates to youth, feels young so acts as such, and quite often does whatever it wants in its own individualistic way without raising ethical issues.

- It is aggressive and impulsive and has lots of vitality, almost like something within refuses to mature.

- The relationship possesses high energies, mainly in their head, as this relationship must always control its internal fights.

- R9 must monitor their impulses and urges, slow down, and listen more efficiently.

- The relationship often relates to medicine, therapy, healing, psychology, and the soul.

- The relationship is very sensual and sexual.

- This relationship is all about freedom.

Basic energY traits of each Year

Basic Energy Traits of Each Year

The main energy of each year in your life can also be predictable. We can find out about the energy of any year. Here's how: add the sum of the *month* and the *day* of the birth date to the sum of the *year* you are in, or better, to the sum of the year you are interested in (the energy of the year is calculated from birthday to birthday) calculated to one digit.

For example, if today is a day in December 2007, and we are interested in knowing the energy for a person named Sara in August 2008, we will have to calculate the energy according to a specific order. Just add and sum up the day and the month of her birth date, together with the sum of the year we are interested in knowing.

Assuming that Sara's birth date is 23 October, we make October (the tenth month of the year) equal 10.

So, 2 + 3 + 10 = 15, and then 1 + 5 = **6**

Excellent!

Now, look at the month of Sara's birthday. Her last birthday was in October 2007, and therefore she is still under the year's influence of her last birthday.

Great!

Now, add the sum of the month plus the sum of the day of her birth date — 6 — to the sum of the year of her last birthday, which is 2007.

6 + 2 + 0 + 0 + 7 = 15, and then 1 + 5 = **6**

In fact, six will represent the energy code number of the year that Sara is in 2007. Then in October 2008, Sara's energy would be influenced the entire year by the energy of number seven.

2 + 3 + 10 + 2 + 0 + 0 + 8 = 25, and then 2 + 5 = **7**

Now using this same information, we can calculate any energy from her past. Let us calculate, for example, how the year 2004 was for Sara, energetically speaking.

2 + 3 (her day of birth) + 1+ 0 (October) + 2 + 0 + 0 + 4 (year of interest) = 12, and then 1 + 2 = **3**

A person enters the new energy approximately a month or two before his or her birth date. It depends on the person's energy.

This amazing knowledge helps us to predict and plan better for the future based on the character and traits that are part of each number and therefore of each year.

It would be beneficial for us to calculate and find out other people's energy of the year. That will give you a clear indication as to where that person is headed and at what point and time that individual is at any given moment in life and what would most likely be the energy/things that the person will do, experience, and feel.

Knowledge gives us the ability to advance in life with much freedom and ease; therefore, use it often and use it wisely!

Basic Traits of The Energy of Year Number One (Y1)

- In this year, we can expect numerous new things, the beginning of new things, and openings of a new cycle of life. Therefore, it can be an excellent year for a new career or business, relocating, or whatever relates to new beginnings and personal growth.

- This year has a male tone to it. The person with this energy feels and acts in a more masculine way by providing, doing, creating, giving, and building.

- There is an individualistic self-development and growth flavor to this year.

- An increase of vitality and self-esteem is highly expected in this year.

- The person in this year receives all the right help and support to accomplish all set goals in an easier and faster way.

- The energy of being the number one (a leading number), may make you feel good and in control, but you will forget to include the people you love and care about. It is a "me, me, me, and all about me" year. Therefore, some loneliness may be associated with this year.

- You will give special focus and attention to the youth of the house or one you love. Special or different attention will be given to them since it is related to the "all about me" attitude.

- Self-love grows and is in the air. Keep it up and use it wisely. This is a great time to plan for the next nine years, at least!

- Remember, it is your year, and it is all about you, so enjoy leading your life the right way.

Basic Traits of The Energy of Year Number Two (Y2)

- This year is extremely different and unique in so many ways. In fact, this year you can expect the energy to be wrapped around the house, the family, relationships, dealing with motherhood issues, or a birth.

- In this year, you will find a stronger need to care for others, and you will be able to feel and understand others like never before.

- *Warning*! There is excess sensitivity this year, so lighten up! Let go of the words and things that hurt you, for you are more likely to take things personally and get offended easily.

- Watch your weight and financial situation carefully since your emotional state of mind may influence them.

- In this year, there is a tendency to spend lots of time at home with family and friends, eating, socializing, or simply feeling good and cozy with all that is familiar.

- This year strongly relates to the past, and therefore things from the past may be a flavor of this year.

- It is a relationship year and is known as the soul mate year. You will more likely meet your soul mate if single, or experience more romanticism if in a relationship.

- It is an extremely fruitful and productive year.

- Try to spend more time out of the house even if you have to delegate some of your responsibilities to others, for this year tends to bring you home in so many great ways. Make a point to be strong, healthy, and emotionally balanced.

Basic Traits of The Energy of Year Number Three (Y3)

- This year is extremely different from the one that preceded it. In this year, you will feel pulled out of the house a lot. You will spend most of your time traveling, in nature, or simply in the outdoors.

- There is an urge that pushes you to freedom, study, spiritual growth, self-expression, and exposing one's talents.

- It is an active year filled with traveling, adventuring, and going and coming with a schedule. It is imperative that you remember to focus and stay organized. Being organized will help you keep and complete your goals.

- This year relates to spaces and a sense of freedom. It also relates to justice. People in this year may find that they are often defending others.

- You will love the way you feel, for your heart is open and optimistic. You will feel freedom flowing in and out of you. I associate and relate optimism and openness to the high (probability) chance of winning in this year.

- The year brings winning and rewards in whatever you associate yourself with. Therefore, think big, dare, and take the right chances. It is a freedom year!

Basic Traits of The Energy of Year Number Four (Y4)

- This year is completely different from the one that preceded it, mainly since it represents a turning point in the way you conduct yourself. It brings you to break old patterns and limiting thoughts.

- In fact, it lets you break from the way you have acted, felt, and dealt with things, and will lead you toward independence with a strong, powerful, and focused vision toward the future.

- This year has an individualistic character, and you will find yourself searching for your soul's purpose and direction. You will let go of the one you followed, for it will be considered part of the past, which you will easily let go.

- Yes, you will reinvent yourself in a unique way that truly suits your individuality.

- This year relates to inventions, something new, positive and unexpected news, opportunities, advancements, and technologies that promote stepping to high rank or social life and letting go of the old.

- This year you will also experience freedom and joy from socializing, democracy, technology, flights, knowledge, and the great breakthroughs it brings.

Basic Traits of The Energy of Year Number Five (Y5)

- The years from one to four were all about growing, learning, and experiencing things that relate to our doing, while year number five is all about communicating and expressing the changes and wisdom acquired.

- Enjoy a great social outgoing time where you look and feel good. You feel informed and connected to information and knowledge while you express and communicate your own wisdom.

- In fact, this year you will be subjected to the complexity of things or information that will be easily processed, and you will be able to understand and relate to complex information that in other years (numbers) you would have had difficulties to understand.

- This year brings you to take the stage and garner attention. You attract publicity in a natural way, so enjoy a positive one. Stay away from gossip and other negative communication even if someone drags you into it.

- Be a better listener and communicate with love all that you desire or know.

- Articulation, action, and movement are part of this number, and will be a part of the year too.

- Often you will be doing or dealing with several things all at once, though some of these things will serve as distractions. Ask yourself why you are doing that. Are you distracting yourself? Why? What would you do differently?

- Since this is a communicative year, most of the energy is mental; therefore, make it a point to do some physical activities, which will easily release any negativity and improve your mental capabilities.

- This year is about you. You are under the spotlight; therefore, make the best out of it and shine like the star that you are.

Basic Traits of The Energy of Year Number Six (R6)

- It is a beautiful year in that it deals with beauty—the exterior, looking good, creation, and perfection.

- In this year, you will attract the perfect relationship or partnership. With your ability to communicate and attract relationships, you will find yourself having to do with "she/he did, I said" that are common in dealing and having issues with relationships.

- This year raises questions: Who are you in this relationship? What is your share? What is your part in it all? Therefore, the year pushes you to commit and give form and conditions to your relationships.

- The previous year was social but mainly communicative. This year is all about being social and looking good in the eyes of everyone, being displayed or put on display. Looking good often involves the use of makeup, new colors, style, and design.

- If you are single this year, it will push you to look for a partner. It is also a soul mate year, as the soul pushes you to display yourself and be open. The year leads to committed relationships with a great ability to negotiate the perfect terms, needs, and conditions.

- It is an artistic and creative year, yet you are required to remember to stay focused.

- You will experience and use colors and designs for decorating yourself, your work, your home, or you will be using it in your work.

- Most of the attention is on the exteriority of things and the way they look, instead of working on and from within. Knowing it, being aware of it, and remembering it is the key to a successful year. In the meanwhile, enjoy the great hospitality and the social, romantic, and outgoing year.

Basic Traits of The Energy of Year Number Seven (R7)

- This year is taking a subconscious and unexpected turn from the way you lived the previous year. Assuming you focused entirely on relationships and appearances, this year you will start to go inward, questioning your inner soul about your life and lifestyle.

- This year you will feel a strong energy that joins you from above, be it your soul or the divine. This energy will guide you as to the things you need to do, achieve, and change and you will most likely do it.

- Some say this is a correction year. A special angel comes down, joins you, and helps you do the things that your soul knows and feels obligated to do and change, yet it was extremely hard for you to do until now. The things that are so hard for us to do give us hints regarding the so-called corrections that we came here to perform.

- Seven is a powerful number and always relates to joined energies. We easily and naturally enjoy this added energy every seventh day of the week, which is Shabbat according to the laws of creation.

- This year is powerful, spiritual, and composed of events charged with strong emotions that always push the individual to self-discovery, improvements, and personal development especially for and from the soul.

- You may experience feelings of missing out on things, yet remember those are only feelings. Use the strong and divine energy that is within you this year to change and transform the feelings to growth and achieve positive change.

143

- This year is strong; therefore, deal with it and enjoy the wonderful and successful outcomes. Avoid trying to escape any uncomfortable feelings with sleep, food, drugs, alcohol, or any other abusive and addicted way, which is typical and a natural part of the energy of the year, for when you are numbed, you disconnect from your soul.

- This year is unique and special since you get all the right help and divine support.

Basic Traits of The Energy of Year Number Eight (Y8)

- The year is moving from the spiritual energy and changes from within the soul to a more conservative and realistic one.

- The entire year, you will find yourself wrapped around your career, life, work, and profits. At times, this year may feel heavy or loaded with responsibility and obligations, but it is always an extremely profitable year.

- The main trait of the number eight is its inability to accept and see different solutions than the one used traditionally to solve and deal with the issues at hand. Therefore, just like the shape of the eight, you will find yourself dealing with the same things (even if we are talking about good things) over and over again. It will feel like you cannot get out of the situation, which can make this year feel somewhat heavy.

- The good news is that when you reach this year, you reached it with a sense of maturity and wisdom and therefore it is a rewarding year financially too.

- Particular traits will help you to push through this year and climb the ladder to increase or improve your social status, hierarchy, and reach your goals easier and faster than you imagined. This is also because you will be doing all the right things to reach your goals, especially the financial ones, even if it means long hours of focused work.

- Remember, it always relates to profits, and therefore it pays out great profits.

- Thanks to the maturity level, which now combines with orthodox or conservative energy, you may feel compelled or pulled toward marriage and other forms of traditional and conservative ceremonies.

- This is your time to lead your life with the right boundaries. What seems a conservative way is actually, according to the laws and rules, always rewarding!

- Enjoy the rewards and profits from your labor and right doing with the right intentions. In other words, whatever you do in this year, will turn out rewarding and extremely profitable for you.

Basic Traits of The Energy of Year Number Nine (Y9)

- This year possesses a strong and powerful energy.

- You will focus on details instead of the big picture. This is actually good for you since this year is a kind of a cleanup year—a year to clean out the little things that can clutter your life.

- This is a cleanup from what is old and unnecessary. This process is vital for year number one where you will begin a new cycle of another nine years.

- Extreme strength, decisiveness, and aggressiveness are the energies of the year. You will deal with things from your past and will have to make the right and necessary closures to terminate and let go of the things, relationships, situations, beliefs, traits, and projects that are too painful, old, or simply unimportant.

- Needs to monitor and control the strong internal conflicts that may otherwise turn into aggressive energy.

- This year you should tone down your stress levels and know that it may not mean that you have to give up the relationship in question; you simply could give up on one of your old traits that reflect a painful, destructive, or negative belief that may attract the stress.

- This year you may find yourself more rebellious, independent, impulsive, childish, and somewhat selfish.

- This year relates to music, dancing, passion, sexuality, and sensual feelings. It also relates to youth and staying or feeling young and childlike.

- Enjoy the strong and powerful connection and passion to and from life during this amazing and powerful year.

- Use love, compassion, and patience as your guide and exercise out any aggression—physically and emotionally.

Part III

Exterior Codes

The Basic Energy Traits of The Spaces You own, rent, lease, stay, work, reside, and lodge in

———◆◆◆———

Knowing the energy of the house, office, room, restaurant, car, ship, plane, or any other location and space that you own or spend time in, is extremely important since your energy may be influenced by it as well. In addition, you might choose—consciously or subconsciously—the specific energy in order to achieve one or more of your goals, so enjoy the wonderful outcomes.

We can discover the energy of the place/space we are interested in by calculating the numerical values of the letters and/or the numbers representing the address of the place or the identification of the place.

The most important numbers for you to know and calculate (when calculating a real estate property, for example) are the numbers you see on the entrance door, for that is the main number that may influence you.

Once you know the number and the energy associated with it, you can either like it or keep it. Alternatively, you can choose the energy and the number that includes the desired energy that you do like or desire, and change it whenever you want to the one desired.

There are two ways, according to my knowledge and experience, to change the energy in your home, office, hotel room, studio, class, etc. The first way is to change the energy by *physically relocating or moving* to a place that already owns the desired energy.

The second alternative, which I personally find easier—it gives the ability to change at any given moment without creating major unnecessary movement and relocation—is to create the desired change by *consciously, intentionally, and physically* changing, removing, or adding a number. This number, when added to the rest of the numbers already on the door, will sum up to the one-digit number that you desire. This is similar to the process of adding a name or a letter to a name.

For example, if you look for an office space or a location for your business, look for a number one, three, five, six, or eight depending on the type of business. (Be sure to add a number that would sum up to the desired number.) If you are working with the law, beauty, or money, the numbers three, six, and nine are excellent choices.

I know the second option may seem unreal or stupid. I have heard comments from people, but once they experienced how the energy worked for them in their properties, they attested how great and magically it works!

You too may have a similar opinion if you have not tried the numeric code of energy, yet I have a feeling that after you try it for yourself, you will be able to see, feel, and acknowledge the positive energy change within the place of your choice without having to relocate.

Knowing the energy of the numbers is helpful in so many levels, but first you need to know or decide in advance what you want to have, achieve, receive, and accomplish from each place or space in your life. Knowing the intention and purpose you have from each person, thing, or space in your life is powerful, for only when you know it, can you truly have it and enjoy it!

In the next few pages, you will discover the natural traits of the space according to its numeric value. Read, think, and decide what kind of energy you want in your life. Go ahead; calculate the numeric code of energy in the spaces that you most spend your time in.

The Basic Energy Traits of Space/ Place Number One (SP1)

- Is famous or well known and always relates to pride and status since it is mostly famous or belongs to someone who is famous.

- It creates a competitive atmosphere.

- Often makes the people living in the space or place associated by the number one, feel a strong need to lead and to be number one in all their undertakings, and they achieve outstanding accomplishments.

- Is noticeable, eye-catching, and attracts a lot of attention, help, support, and promotions.

- Is a great place for children.

- Is good, unique, positive, and has lively energy.

- The space is an excellent provider, is financially secure, and attracts money naturally.

- Attracts many people, is hospitable, entertains guests, loves parties, and is creative.

- Is a great place for children, for entertaining, for business, and investment.

- Has a tendency to be a home/office/business for leaders, lawyers, artists, teachers, schools, stars, or famous people.

The Basic Energy Traits of Space/ Place Number Two (SP2)

- Always relates to family and to what is familiar and known.

- Gives a great feeling of love and comfort, and people always feels at home, catered, and cared for. Great hospitality, cooking, and serving lots of food becomes a way of life.

- There is a lot of sharing and taking care of others, although it would be wise to watch out for overspending, overeating, oversensitivity, and jealousy.

- Is manipulative, uses different forms of manipulation, and therefore keeps secrets or just "keeps the dirt under the rug."

- Due to its female energy, it attracts children and pregnancies. Motherhood, or issues with a mother figure, is a dominant factor of the place.

- Has energy of constant transformation; watch out for burglars since it may attract jealousy.

- Is creative and attracts imaginative and productive people.

- It may manifest sensitivity in the form of liquid issues and leaks.

- Is a great space for schools, healing, therapy, or food centers.

The Basic Energy Traits of Space/ Place Number Three (SP3)

- It gives a feeling of freedom and expansion as well as being spacious and bright.

- It attracts people who love to spend their time outdoors in nature and with animals. Most of the outdoor activity will allow people to do things to reach their goals and expand their vision.

- It represents a powerful energy that pushes for outdoor adventures, traveling, and living life to the fullest.

- The space/place is open, warm, positive, and loving, even if it may appear cold at times.

- The space/place will create an ambiance of positive feelings that will lead to great ideas.

- It has a type of studying and mental expansion kind of energy.

- Relates to laws and justice and a feeling of what's right.

- Is a great place for lawyers, import-export businesses, delivering and transporting of things, businesspeople, advisers, counseling, teachers, or athletic and active people.

The Basic Energy Traits of Space/ Place Number Four (SP4)

- It has a new or modern look, feel, and design.

- It tends to use new and modern furniture as a reminder of its liberal energy.

- Always appears fresh, bright, and separated from the past.

- Attracts democratic, generous, and open-minded people or pushes people to be free, democratic, generous, and to conduct themselves in an unlimited guilt-free life.

- It provides the feeling that everything is allowed.

- The place/space creates an environment that is extremely social, and it has a strong unitary purpose.

- It looks for and attracts new technology or information of higher intellect.

- Attracts its own unique routine and discipline, which might be unusual to many.

- Relates to heights, and therefore the person who occupies the space will have to do with heights. The people or person in this environment is most likely a frequent flyer, is located next to an airport, or lives in a high-rise.

- Is a great place for independent work, watching the stars, for pilots, airports, research, inventions, technology, and for known upscale or modern locations.

The Basic Energy Traits of Space/Place Number Five (SP5)

- Has a tendency to induce habits of being constantly busy.

- It is noisy, mainly thanks to the modes of transportation, ringing phones, faxes coming in, and many people moving in and out, especially young ones.

- It constantly attracts complex communication and high intelligence.

- Makes the people who occupy the space look and feel younger, and in turn, it attracts many intelligent young people.

- It is always involved in education and learning.

- Is busy and restless and attracts a lot of fame.

- Is about communication constantly and in so many creative ways (mainly positive, for it relates to positive thinking also).

- Is spiritual but also material and attracts them both.

- Is a great place for schools, teachers, consultants, healers, traders, stars, movie theaters, clubs, as well as for whatever deals with modes of transportation (car dealerships, boat stores, airports, and so much more).

- It is also great for stores and businesses that communicate a status, a fate, an idea, or a belief.

The Basic Energy Traits of Space/ Place Number Six (SP6)

- It focuses on art, decor, beauty, and the physical appearance of those within its walls as well as the place itself.

- It attracts terrific hospitality, lots of meals, and people coming and going often.

- Has harmony that is easily felt.

- Has a romantic and sexual atmosphere.

- It makes the people within the space number six attractive, intelligent, and good negotiators.

- The place/space encourages individuals to attract marriage, partnerships, and relationships.

- It gives the majority of its inhabitants a strong sense of judgment and in expressing their opinions even in those matters that do not directly concern them.

- It has a strong sense of creativity and insights.

- Is a great place for business people, counselors, diplomats, politicians, lawyers, beauticians, fashion designers, interior designers, decorators, painters, and writers. It can become spas, art centers, fashion homes, publishing homes, government centers, etc.

The Basic Energy Traits of Space/ Place Number Seven (SP7)

- Simple, quiet, spiritual, modest, and creative, and owns many unique art items.

- Often of silence, with its main energy the feeling that something is weird and different, and at times even odd.

- It gives the feeling of eternity, which explains the difficulty in changing, selling, or moving away.

- Always has to do with healing, psychology, sociology, and spirituality. It also relates to the development and well-being of the soul and society.

- Relates to the realm of the angels, and at times may feel as if there is an additional energy in the place or simply heavy feelings as if the energy is stuffed.

- Makes people in this space feel the need to escape emotions in many ways. Therefore, they must watch out and monitor any negative addictions or abuse such as alcohol, drugs, oversleeping, overeating, or overspending.

- Highly appreciates peace and quiet even if at times the people within these walls feel as if they compromise or receive less than what they truly deserve in exchange.

- It may also experience issues with the energy levels of the place or of the people within that space, which will manifest with concerns or problems with the electric circuit, flow/supply, appliances, or devices, as well as with dizziness or weakness.

- It makes a great place for advising, teaching, psychology, healing, or social work as well as for meetings, gatherings, socializing, preaching, partying, or bars.

The Basic Energy Traits of Space/ Place Number Eight (SP8)

- The space/place represents social status and hierarchy.

- Often gives the feeling of limitations, fatalism, heaviness, realism, concreteness, the old-fashioned, and religiosity (maybe even the orthodox kind).

- Has a tendency to reflect and attract heaviness, limitation, and seriousness, as well as feelings of judgment, guilt, and obligations.

- It is usually decorated with massive and old-fashioned (and less joyful) furniture.

- Pushes reality and seriousness in the environment to take over and at times may feel it is missing joy, laughter, and music.

- Just like the shape of the number eight, infinity deals with similar issues/ problems or matters over and over again, giving the inhabitants the feeling of constantly repeating their actions and that of going up and down without the ability to break free, a fact that may induce the emotion of feeling stuffed or clogged.

- The space/place is often well known for being productive and profitable even if it most likely happens through hard work or long periods of hard work.

- It succeeds through discipline, hard work, commitment, and boundaries.

- Is a great place for restaurants, accounting, banking, praying, teaching, and consulting.

The Basic Energy Traits of Space/ Place Number Nine (SP9)

- Highly energetic and often filled with people whom feel and look dynamic and young.

- Has a lot of things happening all at once and in a unique way.

- Attracts argumentative, rebellious, and anxious people or situations.

- Lets strong feelings such as selfishness, being materialistic, being opinionated, and righteousness experienced at times by the people within the space.

- Witnesses a constant ending of things—relationships or old projects and a beginning of new ones. (It is amazing, this process happens in great detail!)

- Gives a strong sense of freedom, independence, and individualism.

- Often relates to sports in general and to an aerobic type in particular.

- Often motivated by a free spirit and a sense of immorality; the people within the space often feel like doing whatever they want.

- Promotes creativity, sensuality, sexuality, precision, perfection, and judgment.

- Is a great place for lawyers, accountants, healers, dancers, musicians, and artists. The space can become law offices, courthouses, gyms, weight loss centers, dancing schools, hospitals, etc.

Basic Energy Traits of Your Cars, Jet Skis, Yacht, Boat and Your Airplane

As I mentioned earlier, your energy is mainly influenced by your name, birth date, and relationships, as well as by the energy of the space you are in or are using. Therefore, you are also influenced by the space of the mode of transportation you use (according to its number from 1 to 9) such as cars, aircraft (flight), Jet Skis, boats, cruises, etc.

The different modes of transportation represent a space that has a name and a number as identification. The plate number identifies the energy and its purposes.

In the following pages, I will briefly guide you to the traits and energies you will feel when you are in these spaces. Here again, add all the numbers to obtain a one-digit number on the plate, tag, seat, flight number, or any other number that is marking the space. (When both letters and numbers are used, calculate only the numbers.)

Once again, add the numbers, and then discover the energy of the mode of transportation.

The Basic Energy Traits of the Mode of Transportation Number One (T1)

- Relates to status and hierarchy and always attracts lots of attention.

- Cares for and strives to make a good impression.

- Is driven well, and the driver feels like a pro driving the vehicle.

The Basic Energy Traits of the Mode of Transportation Number Two (T2)

————— ·•·•· —————

- Is normally loved by people for the trip, and it gives them the feeling of warmth and comfort.

- Is great on the road and rarely has any problems; however, if any arises, it involves dealing with liquids.

- It is used mainly for family trips or purposes.

The Basic Energy Traits of the Mode of Transportation Number Three (T3)

- Accumulates high mileage due to its innate want to travel.

- Has a lack of focus.

- Is a safe mode of transportation, and the driver feels good and safe driving it.

- Is a comfortable mode of transportation that enjoys successful and rewarding travel.

- Is owned or driven by someone who basically studies, works, eats, and does almost everything in that mode of transportation.

- It is an excellent means of transportation that needs very little work or maintenance.

- Always has something going on that enriches the travel.

- Is a mode of transportation with lots of luck. The people within feel mostly safe and blessed, perhaps because the number three possesses a positive attitude.

The Basic Energy Traits of the Mode of Transportation Number Four (T4)

- Is unpredictable because it constantly attracts, invents, and creates new things (mainly good things, thanks to its mainly positive energy).

- Appears to look like it is flying, for it is known to be extremely fast.

- Attracts new technologies and inventions, and maybe that is the reason it requires visits to the mechanic often.

The Basic Energy Traits of the Mode of Transportation Number Five (T5)

- Is a great ride, giving great feelings, and is always traveling, moving, or active.

- Revolves around intelligent driving, fun, and communication with lots of information given.

- Not very flashy, somewhat modest, and well kept.

- Rarely has mechanical issues and is very dependable.

The Basic Energy Traits of the Mode of Transportation Number Six (T6)

- Is a good-looking car or it is excessively decorated with all the nice little gadgets. You see the passion of color, design, and exterior beauty of the number six.

- Used for short, cozy, and loving rides.

- This transportation attracts situations of intense feelings, mainly those of love; however there may be anger and misunderstanding from others regarding the driver.

- Attracts and deals with partnerships, relationships, or situations.

The Basic Energy Traits of the Mode of Transportation Number Seven (T7)

- Is a unique and a misleading car in many ways.

- Will usually look like one thing and then be the exact opposite.

- Is recommended to be given special attention and to check all the information given to you before making any purchases.

- Deals with or relates to healing, psychology, therapy, or development of the soul.

- Has an engine that is stronger than expected.

The basic Energy Traits of the Mode of Transportation Number Eight (T8)

- Relates to status and hierarchy, and in fact, is used mainly by businesspeople to work and represents them and their status in life.

- Is expensive to buy and maintain, but it is always profitable, because at the end, it produces great profits.

- Attracts and creates mixed feelings.

The Basic Energy Traits of the Mode of Transportation Number Nine (T9)

———————

- Has hot energy, dark colors, and travels less.

- Is somewhat possessed with aggressive energy.

- Is used by people who are mostly youthful, young, or dynamic and usually for short trips.

- Has a sense of individualism, and therefore attracts an aggressive, rebellious, childish, and selfish attitude.

Part IV

Other Significant
nu mBers——Codes

Other Significant Numbers—Codes!

Have you ever wondered if random numbers given to you might be meaningful in one way or another? Well, I believe they are. They give a specific indication as to the cause and purpose as well as to the things, feelings, or actions that you will be doing, experiencing, controlling, or changing while holding or using the thing, service, privilege, or identification of the number given.

Confused? Well, a few examples of random numbers are significant, for they hold the code or the secret of their purpose and the way they express themselves in a person's life.

For example: a social security number, a driver's license number, a bank account number, a student ID number, a movie ticket number, a telephone number, etcetera. It could be a number you get when you stand in line for something, when you participate in a competition, or a number that marks a test or an examination.

I began following random numbers and studied how their energy affects or manifests in the lives of people. I realize that these numbers may seem casual or serve to keep a certain order for the institute or the place that gives out the numbers. However, they too are significant and meant for much more than that since they represent certain energies.

Begin calculating the given numbers in your life by adding them to a one-digit number. When numbers and letters are together, calculate *only* the numbers.

For example, here is a driver's license number: R-654-

073-3, which adds up as

$6 + 5 + 4 + 0 + 7 + 3 + 3 = 28$, then $2 + 8 = 10$, and then $1 + 0 = 1$.

Once you achieve a one-digit sum of the random number, you can read about its energy, traits, and purpose in the following pages.

175

Number one will bring you to

- Strive to be the number one in all things, to compete, and to have strong ambitions.

- Desire and attract love, power, money and respect Naturally and easily.

- Have strong passion for leadership and to be positively well known, appreciated, desired, praised, glorified, recognized, and much more, and you will achieve it all easily.

- Be unique, creative, artistic, romantic, protective, loving, and charismatic, but also incredibly mature and demanding.

- Transform, become, or develop a masculine to the personality.

- Receive the right help needed to achieve any goal naturally and easily, something that leads to success and leadership.

- Well known—publicity and exposure and to shine just like the sun for the self and others.

- Be or become an excellent provider for the self and others.

- Experience some emotions of loneliness, pride, and egotism. It will be best if these are monitored, controlled, and communicated with others on a humble level. Share and include others more often and allow them to feel adequate.

Number two will bring you to

- Be dependent on things, circumstances, or people for energy, love, support, advice, and success.

- Deal with low self-esteem, self-validation, and seeking approval from others.

- Be extremely sensitive and therefore to feel, understand, and care for others.

- Be or assume to be a mother figure with all that it means and represents, since number two carries feminine traits such as great receivers.

- Be, transform, or become more feminine, sensual, passionate, and rich with fantasy and imagination.

- Have high intuition that is mostly felt in the stomach.

- Be nurturing, sensitive, and family-oriented, yet may have some issues with selected members of the family or society, especially with a mother figure.

- Be more at home (or indoors) and less out in the public.

- Be connected and related to the past.

- Be extremely sensitive that may lead to overeating.

Number three will bring you to

- Looking forward and into the future and completely detached from the past. You will cultivate and hold a bigger vision and a positive attitude.

- Be or desire freedom and expansion of all kinds. In fact, it will bring you to expand in spiritual, material, or philosophical matters, or in terms of distance or simply in knowledge and awareness.

- Enjoy the outdoors and open spaces.

- Be rewarded and a winner.

- Take appropriate steps and risks to achieve your goals.

- Become daring and intuitive and to attract good luck and other rewards.

- Deal with a strong sense of justice and a need or desire to protect and/or represent someone or represent the law in one form or another.

- Has difficulty committing to others and things, as it loves its freedom. Has difficulty focusing and completing things until the end while paying attention to the details required.

- At time may appear or act careless and cold to others.

Number four will bring you to

- Be special, original, and innovative.

- Look further for unique solutions or ways to express your being.

- Have the ability to find solutions or ideas easily and therefore to invent and improvise.

- Relate to the new, modern, and maybe even the unexpected.

- Easily let go of the past and have no regrets or guilt feelings.

- Do whatever you want without raising ethical questions.

- Associate and relate to technology, electronic devices, and anything that has to do with the media, publicity, and TV.

- Relate to levels and heights, and therefore to flights, great visions, high social ranks, high energy, be highly paid as well as be and feel high in the head, and therefore must work on keeping grounded.

- Be social, loving, and loved by most. Needs and wants people and family, but wants to love and keep the freedom and independence as a number one priority.

- Be and express the self in a free and independent way.

- It relates to super intelligence.

Number five will bring you to

- Movement and traveling, having a positive attitude, relating to beauty, spirituality, and the material.

- Enjoy being with others, communicating, and sharing knowledge.

- Be on the move, either traveling or feeling restless and always relating to modes of transportation.

- Be communicative, creative, and often of higher intellect.

- Be articulate and have a great ability to comprehend complex information.

- Be a speaker, which will bring you to teach, act, trade, sing, or anything else that uses the art of communication.

- Understand the connection between mind, body, and soul.

- Be young at soul and to look and feel younger.

- Associate and feel more comfortable with those of the younger generation.

- Gets bored easily and therefore handles multiple tasks all at once.

- Be easily distracted and remembers to stay focused and completes all started projects, avoids gossip, and negative communication.

Number six will bring you to

- Relate to beauty, color, decorating, and looking great.

- Be in harmony and beautiful, giving more attention to outer beauty than inner beauty.

- Have difficulties to be alone; therefore, you will look to others and attract friends, relationships, and partnerships of different kinds.

- Be a great negotiator and listener and to understand people and situations.

- Focus and appreciate beauty and the material world (will always attract material things).

- Look for peace and tranquility, and get along well with others.

- Feel connected with other people and enjoy participating in something bigger and stronger.

- Relate to color, makeup, design, decoration, and art.

- Relate to harmony, romanticism, passion, and sexuality.

- Provide great hospitality and service.

Number seven will bring you to

- Relate to complex things such as the philosophical, mystical, psychological, spiritual, and the development of the soul.

- Be interested in caring, nurturing, healing, and guiding others even if carrying some feelings of sacrifice or compromises or emotionally closing off feelings.

- Have strong emotional baggage and have to learn to let go of situations and things that are less beneficial to you, especially if related to the past.

- Own a powerful energy that at times turns inward and therefore will be self-destructive.

- Feel the urge to avoid things and situations and a deep need to escape using all kinds of addictions.

- Watch and monitor habits, addictions, weaknesses, and a lack of energy, for they are possible.

- Desire to be a part of something or to belong to something—a group, philosophy, or someone.

- Have identity issues internally.

- Feel one is sacrificing and even missing out on things such as doing business.

- Be forgiving and loving and to represent eternity.

- Possess a strong ability to heal and help others.

Number eight will bring you to

- Be mature, responsible, and determined as well as to possess a unique drive.

- Have a career, hierarchy, and management as number one priorities.

- Push to reach set goals no matter what it takes.

- Love to be in control.

- Test others and the self and do it constantly with no shortcuts or discounts.

- Be and act in a conservative, traditional, and maybe orthodox or religious way.

- Desire to be well known, to reach a certain status and name, and to desire fame, boundaries, and hierarchy.

- Work hard and for long periods.

- Do it all alone without asking for help from anyone even if it means long periods of hardship with difficulties to change circumstances. Accept destiny and bring the self to live in harmony with the Creator.

- Develop and build, yet forgetful of its interior.

- Be realistic and to relate to musts and should dos.

- Stress out regarding authority.

- Be profitable even if it takes hard work.

Number nine will bring you to

- Experience strong physical energies and the need to lead and be the first in everything.

- Be competitive, childish, and often independent as well as selfish.

- Individualism, rebelliousness, and dislike of hierarchy and authority.

- Have a strong passion for dancing and freedom of any kind, especially of self-expression and creativity.

- Feel young or relate to youth and act like one.

- Do everything in a unique and individualistic way without raising ethical issues.

- Be aggressive and impulsive with lots of vitality, almost like something within refuses to mature.

- Be sensual and sexual yet also relate to medicine, therapy, healing, psychology, and the soul.

- Have minor justice "wars "or disagreements.

- Have conflict of ideas and opinions and insist on them.

- Have situations that require control over impulses and urges making you slow down or listen more.

- Feeling as if you are in a survival mode.

Part V

What is next?

So, What's Next?

Wonderful! Now that you know yourself and others better, the energy of the year you are in and what will follow (the energy of your home, car, yacht, real estate properties, office, airplane, and more) can help to better your life even more. You can continue to call on the right and desired energies and things into your life by using the law of attraction to your favor and that of the people you care about and love.

In the following pages, I will guide you through the right steps to take and introduce you to a magical formula that will create and attract for you whatever you desire in a fast, easy, and safe way.

Here we will go back to the power of the words. Remember? I explained earlier how words call on a specific character and energy that are contained in the name of the things you call. Here we will write down our desires in a form of a letter to the divine, soul mate, parents, etc. We will use the right words to call and create for you all that you desire, and begin to enjoy living the life you want!

The people I taught who applied this technique achieved what they wanted and wished to achieve, they changed, or they attracted things easily and magically. I have a feeling you will love it too. Write your own life script and enjoy the outcome. Once you write it down, you can read it to yourself or others, and then simply let it go. In other words, express your wants and needs, and they will manifest.

It is easy and it works!

The Formula

I can finally share with you this amazing secret. This came from one of the oldest and bestselling life coaching books in history—the Bible. The simplicity of this formula will amaze you, as this information has always been available to us.

The Bible is the ultimate divine book of wisdom; it reveals the precious secrets of life by addressing each area of life through its stories according to the human level of awareness and understanding. It contains the wisdom and the fundamentals of psychology, awareness, health, wealth, sociology, biology, anatomy, physics, math, and so on. It unveils the fundamentals of life and human existence in a basic and timeless book form.

In the first book of the Bible—Genesis—we find the formula which describes how Hashem created everything he did before man was created.

The mystical story of creation holds *the real secret to creating*, which is hidden within. I invite you to take out your Bible and analyze the steps in the formula of creation found in the first chapter of Genesis.

First, Hashem *saw*. It opens with a statement and it describes the situation. "In the beginning the earth was unformed and void. There was darkness everywhere, and the spirit of Hashem hovered over the face of the earth."

Second, Hashem *said*. "Let there be light." This is where he gave the creative command. (Notice the time is in present tense.)

Third, *there was*. Creation was taking place.

Then, Hashem *called it*. Each thing created received a name that gave it energy with its own unique characteristics.

Finally, Hashem saw it was *good*. Therefore, it is a beginning to stage one. This stage represents an ending and the beginning of a new creation.

Now, let us take a closer look at each of these steps. We will see and discover in detail what each step requires and how we can apply it to our daily life.

1. *Saw/see.* This first step is complex because it contains stages 1 and 5 within it. (Notice the time used is both past and present tense.)

   a) See the situation clearly and realistically—the way it is—without tainting your own view upon it, that is, try to make it look better or worse than it actually is. Total *honesty* is the key here, and truthfully accepting it the way it is. This is the meaning of Kabbalah.

   b) Acknowledge how you *feel* about what you see (or the way you see the situation). Next, you have to decide what you actually want to feel and *see* instead (replacing that reality, whichever changes are needed in order for you to be able to take it to the next step).

In other words, visualize a better reality (from where you are) regardless of the actual circumstance, situation, or reality. The best way to start changing a vision is first acknowledge that whatever you see in your life is already a fruit of your own creation. Recognize that you create the reality and characteristics of your life—your side of the street. Essentially, you look at life with a positive attitude and see it as all good.

   c) Cultivate a vision of something good, positive, great, and always better with the highest degree of reality. Cautiously look out for elements, things, or conditions that alter your mood, your senses, or things that may make you see inaccurately as you normally would, such as alcohol and drugs, as well as anger, resentment, fear, alter ego, etc.

On a daily basis, we constantly create our own reality whether we realize it or not. Some people seem to live successful lives and enjoy great abundance of all sorts easily and effortlessly, rightfully and magically. It seems that no matter what they do, they create and attract rewarding events, perfect health, excellent relationships and opportunities, abundance of wealth, joyful outcomes, and feelings, and all the things that they want, love, and enjoy. The reason for such an outcome lies in the practice of this original formula for creation, especially in the second step.

2. *Say/call it.* "God said . . . there was . . . and then God called it."

   a) By assigning a name, it gave the creation all the unique and specific energies, qualities, and characteristics that belong to the name. When we call things, we call on all their unique and specific energies and characteristics. It is all in the words, both negative and positive. Vision is very important, yet the selection and usage of the right *words* is responsible for *creating* the right vision and therefore its manifestation into a reality.

   b) Say clearly and precisely what you want to see manifest without any limitations or doubts. This is what we learn from the next sentence of the formula. For example, when God said, "Let there be light."

   c) Say it aloud or mentally to yourself. Say it, for your mind is speaking constantly; therefore, it also constantly creates for you whether you pay attention to it or not. Point out to yourself and to others what you want your reality to be by expressing it clearly.

   d) Be assertive, use short, *specific, simple, clear,* and *positive* sentences, and words. Avoid using ambiguous words or sentences, and make sure you are correctly understood at all times.

   e) Express and focus only on what you want and desire in your life.

   f) Use the present tense and avoid using the past or future tense. Allow only the present to be referenced when you want to create the future The only time that exists is now!

3. *There was.* Faith, which is the ability to see or know something different and positive is coming or will manifest regardless of the present moment, is the key to success in this step. Trust and simply allow time and space for it to manifest. Be open and accept the reality that you created. Let go of the need to control circumstances, things, and people. Be confident. Feel and know that whatever you asked for is on its way to you already.

From the moment you expressed your wants/needs, it is only a matter of time, which varies and depends on different factors, before you can experience what you asked.

4. *Attitude*: Finally, the creation story ends each day with "And then Hashem saw it was good." Is this statement the end or just the beginning? In fact, the answer to that question is one. This is the ending of what was created while a beginning of a new one. It can be a new beginning of that same one (whatever was already created) or a different one.

This step can be Number 4 as I numbered it in this formula, but it can also be step Number 1, which is about what we see. In fact, the end of each creation, or seeing it and accepting it as good, is not only my recommendation for a good, creative life but is also an important ingredient for success.

The following day, he goes through the same process again. Hashem continues *creating* by seeing and saying.

Now go to the next level and continue to create.

   a) Acknowledge that you have created your reality the way it is right now

   b) Connect to the Creator within you

   c) Firmly believe that you deserve to receive your request

   d) Take the right steps, expect, and accept its manifestation

e) Allow time for its creation, according to what you have requested

f) Acknowledge its manifestation as good

Note that Hashem did not say what he did not want nor did he utter a single word of judgment to the situation. The rule of thumb here is to say only what you want your reality to be. See it manifesting in your life (Step 1) and see it was good and positive.

(Step 4) You have to remember that whatever is or was communicated becomes a reality without any exception or modification.

I am excited to know that my words have power, and that by expressing a combination of words, I connect to the creative force, and create and achieve what I want.

So can you!

In conclusion, when wanting to describe the power of creation, I will say it is easy because *it is in the words*. Words are combinations of letters. We already know from previous chapters that each letter has its own energy and power, traits and character. Thus, when we place them in the right combination, we create words that describe something that has certain characteristics and energies. When we think of or say this word, two things happen at the same time.

First, we see, hear, and/or feel, which translates into pictures and/or feelings. The second thing that happens is that we breathe it in and out of our body and positively influence our entire energy.

Enjoy every day writing your own great, successful, happy, accomplished, rewarding, healthy, and wealthy life story. Enjoy your life the way you want and desire it to be! You are worthy and deserving of all good so enjoy it all! It is good, safe, and easy for you to be happy, healthy, wealthy, important, successful, and all that you were meant to be!

Important Rules That Need Kept in Mind When Writing This Type of Letter or Script/prayer

———————

1. First, begin by looking carefully at your life as it is now. See it clearly — the way things truly are. Accept it as part of your old creation and recognize all the things you wish to change or see changing in your life. Make a list of all the negative things, like relationships or traits you see or experience in your life. Write your list with a pencil so you can easily erase items whenever you are done. Focus on what you tend to attract naturally.

2. Review your list. Decide what you like, what you want to keep, and what you dislike and want to change. Create a new list, the opposite of the negative ones. For example, if in the first list you wrote "abusive," in the second one write "soft, respectful, excellent communicator, gentle," and so on.

3. Start your letter with "Thank you, God, divine, soul mate, or . . . ," for when we give thanks, we are in the state of mind of receiving and/or accepting.

4. Write the letter in the present tense as if it is happening right now. Avoid phrases and words that speak of the past (i.e., looked, came), or future (i.e., will look, will go), for the only time that has power and existence is the present, the now.

5. State everything as a positive affirmation. Write your letter using only positive words. Avoid using negative words in meaning, tone, or in any form or shape such as *no, can't, don't, won't, shouldn't, doesn't, haven't, abusive, liar*, and so on. Using negative affirmations will produce negative results. In addition, this will put a focus on what you do not want, instead of asking

for what you want. Once you finish the letter, read it, and look for negative words. If you find any, *immediately* transform the words into a positive affirmation or goal. For example, if you wrote, "He/she is not fat or not dependent," transform it to the words, "He/she is slim and independent."

6. Be specific; *precision is of the utmost importance.* Write as many details (adjectives) as possible for a perfect manifestation. For example, if you want a pizza with mushrooms, write "pizza with mushrooms." (Omit all the other details such as, "Don't put olives, anchovies, and onions on the pizza.") You simply want a pizza that has thick or thin crispy dough, spicy or mild tomato sauce, Italian portabella mushrooms, and mozzarella kosher or organic or buffalo cheese. Take nothing for granted, even if it seems obvious, unless you are used to receiving everything exactly the way you want it, and so you are open to good surprises.

7. Dare to dream big! Allow your imagination to take you to God's magic land where *all things are possible.* Ask your creative mind to let go of any preconceived limitations. When you connect with the unlimited possibilities, everything is possible and all your dreams, aspirations, and goals will be achieved — thank God.

8. Speak it! Aloud or quietly, but by reading it, you speak to yourself first with the wonderful and powerful creative force. Once you say it, forget about it. Yes, simply know it has begun to manifest in your life whether you believe it or not.

A better understanding of it all takes some practice until you begin to genuinely see it, feel it in your heart, and understand how it works. Soon you will be able to say, "*I know*" instead of "*I believe.*"

Do you see the magical formula hidden in the letter technique?

About the Author

"Asnat Almaliah Frey is a brilliant writer, teacher, spiritual healer, and life coach. She helps thousands of people on a daily basis to achieve their goals whether it is wealth, perfect health, joy, perfect relationships, a sense of accomplishment, balance, ACQUIRE new and positive habits, let go of old and limiting habits, enjoy life and success. She does it through her books, web sites, seminars, products and one on one coaching"

Asnat Almaliah Frey applies channeling, her wisdom, universal laws, meditations; hypnosis, energy work, and shifting consciousness, on a daily basis, to help thousands of individuals achieve their desired outcomes and goals. She knows and uses the right solutions, the correct words, thoughts, and actions that work magic! She helps the individuals to achieve and enjoy a good, fulfilling, happy, healthy, wealthy, and accomplished life, by using their huge and personal potential.

By discovering the true purpose, potential, and opportunities in a person's life, Asnat Almaliah Frey is guiding successfully, rightfully, and easily.

She teaches ways to apply the wonderful laws of the universe to create a positive outcome in a person's life. She enjoys guiding and teaching the thousands and millions of people worldwide through her books, CDs, seminars, coaching services, and websites, as well as through the vast media.

Asnat Almaliah Frey is passionate about her work and seeing the improvements in the lives of her clients. She is an expert in setting and achieving goals and is also passionate about her career mission to help the millions of wonderful people of this wonderful and abundant universe through her books, programs, seminars, one on one coaching, channeling sessions, and more to set the right goals and achieve them rightfully, safely, magically and fast!

In her previous book, *The Message by Jona's No. 5*, the author shares remarkable stories from her life and that of her clients' life. She conveys the message regarding the correct way to attract and create the desired outcome in life rightfully, easily, and safely.

"THE MESSAGE OF HOW TO CREATE AND ACHIEVE WHATEVER YOU WANT IN YOUR LIFE IN A FAST, SAFE, RIGHT, AND EASY WAY IS HERE TO CREATE MAGIC 4U2!"

Made in the USA
Columbia, SC
03 January 2024

29000707R00122